CALLINGTON COMM. COLLEGE.
Photography

AF496570

EXPOSURE CONTROL
IN ENLARGING

EXPOSURE CONTROL
IN ENLARGING

GEORGE L. WAKEFIELD
M.Sc. Tech., Ph.D. F.I.I.P., F.R.P.S.

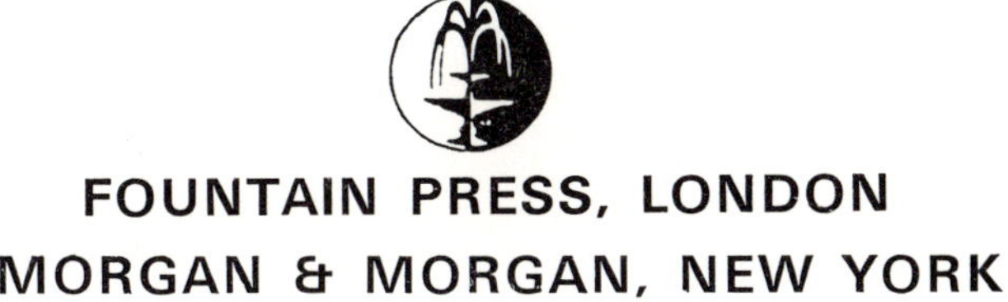

FOUNTAIN PRESS, LONDON
MORGAN & MORGAN, NEW YORK

Fountain Press
46/47 Chancery Lane
London WC2A 1JU.

First Published 1972

ISBN 0 852 42005 6

Set in 11/12 pt. IBM Baskerville printed by photolithography,
and bound in Great Britain at The Pitman Press, Bath

CONTENTS

INTRODUCTION

This book is intended as a practical guide for both amateur and professional photographers who wish to substitute precise measurement for judgement or trial and error methods in arriving at correct exposure times in projection printing.

Some of the theoretical considerations are discussed in the author's book, "Practical Sensitometry" but they have been covered again here to avoid having to refer the reader to another book.

A small proportion of the material has been published in "Amateur Photographer" over a period of years and grateful acknowledgment is made to the publishers of that journal for permission to reproduce it in a more permanent form.

The first and larger section of the text deals with black and white enlarging in which process the use of any kind of meter is comparatively rare. Methods which are unduly time-consuming have been excluded because it is uneconomical to save a sheet of paper costing five pence if it takes labour worth perhaps twenty pence to do it.

Several simple devices are described which can be constructed in a short time by anybody who can use simple tools. Most photographers seem to have the knack of constructing some of their own equipment.

The latter part of the book covers the use of photometry in colour printing mainly for the determination of filter packs for the white light method and also for the estimation of exposure times in white light and tricolour printing.

It can be said with assurance that the use of a photometer in any projection printing process saves time and material and can lead to improved technical quality.

CHAPTER ONE

PRINCIPLES OF PRINTING EXPOSURE ESTIMATION

The sensitometry of making a print from a black and white negative is shown in Figure 1.1. It has to be assumed that we are considering only straightforward printing of normal scenes and that no deliberate tonal distortions are being introduced for the sake of pictorial effect. These are very much a part of practical enlarging and their successful introduction depends on the skill and sensitivity of the photographer. He is greatly assisted however by knowing, in the first instance, the correct basic exposure time. From this he can decide on any local modifications that may be required to darken a shadow here and lighten another there, or to print up a highlight so that it shows gradation that does not appear in a straight print.

In a normal print we expect to see highlights reproduced as nearly white paper and the darkest shadows as approaching the deepest black the paper can give. There are, of course, exceptions to this as in the high or low-key rendering or the misty November landscape. The majority of subjects demand prints in which there is a good black and a clean white and these conditions are satisfied in Figure 1.1. The resulting print is likely to be wholly satisfactory ignoring the possible need for some local shading and printing-up.

If the subject highlights are located too far down on the toe of the printing paper curve where the gradient approaches zero, they will be bald and devoid of gradation. Similarly, there is the liklihood of uniformly black shadows if they are pushed too far up on to the shoulder of the paper curve. It is a commonplace experience to encounter prints with "burnt-out" highlights or "clogged" shadows, or even both together in the same print.

On every paper curve there must be considered to be two limiting points, one on the toe and the other on the shoulder, between which lies the useful exposure range of the paper. Between these points too, measured on the vertical axis, lies

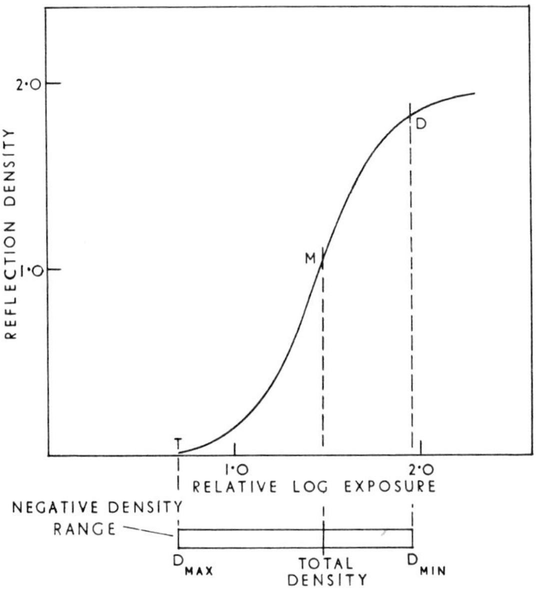

Fig. 1.1 The sensitometry of print making. Shadows and highlights are located at the limiting points on the shoulder and toe of the characteristic curve of the printing paper D and T.

the useful density range of the paper. On average, the highlights and shadows of a print will be located at these two limiting points respectively.

Many attempts have been made to specify methods whereby these two limiting points may be located unequivocally but with no conspicuous success. This is hardly surprising in view of the wide diversity of subjects finding their ways in front of the camera and the varying importance of shadow detail and highlight gradation, depending on the kind of subject and on the rendering required of it.

Despite these variations it is desirable to have some generally-accepted method for specifying the limiting points on the characteristic curve of a printing paper and following from this the magnitude of the exposure range of the material. American Standard Ph 2 : 2—1966, "Sensitometry of Photographic Papers" specifies a method for locating the limiting points on the paper curve and evaluating the log exposure range. This Standard is a revision of A.S. Ph 2 : 2—1953 in which the method of evaluating the exposure range was considerably different. This difference is an indication of the difficulty that exists in finding a universally applicable method of locating the limiting points on the curve.

The main provisions of A.S. Ph 2 : 2—1966 are shown in Figure 1.2. The limiting point on the toe of the curve is at a density of 0.04 above base plus fog density. The upper limiting point is located where the density is 0.9 of the maximum density. The latter is specified as being at a point where the gradient has fallen to 0.05 but it is sufficient to take the absolute maximum density attained by the curve.

Between these specified points, measured on the log exposure axis, is the log exposure range of the paper. Measuring between the same two points, but on the density axis, gives the effective density range of the paper. This depends very much on the surface of the paper and is highest for glossy paper and lowest for smooth matt.

Referring back to Figure 1.1 it will be seen that the density range of the negative is equal to the log exposure range of the paper and such agreement is essential for high-quality prints unless a deliberately distorted tone reproduction is wanted. It is claimed for A.S. Ph 2 : 2—1966 that the method of determining log exposure range gives good correlation with the density range of negatives suitable for printing on the paper concerned.

The various grades of printing papers differ only as regards their exposure ranges as a low-contrast negative calls for a paper with a small log exposure range and a contrasty negative — large density range — has to be printed on a paper with a large log exposure range. (Figure 1.3).

To create the situation shown in Figure 1.1 it is necessary to adjust the printing exposure so that the D_{min} of the negative is recorded at the upper limiting point on the paper curve and the D_{max} at the lower limiting point. In determining exposures in enlarging, the time required is governed

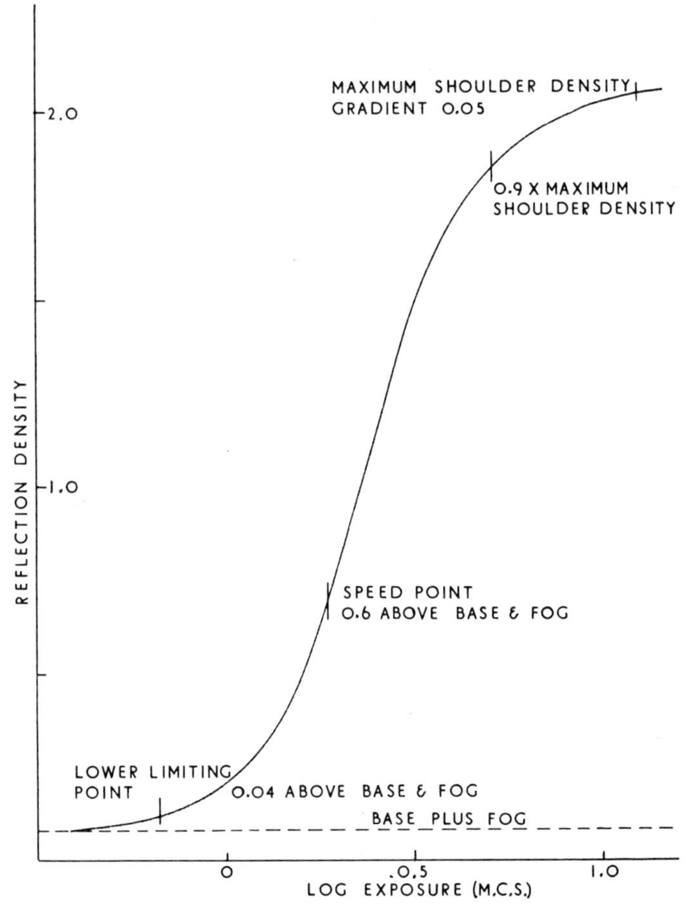

Fig. 1.2 *The limiting points on the characteristic curve of a printing paper as defined in American Standard Ph2: 2–1966.*

by the illumination falling on the easel and the speed of the paper emulsion. If the latter is known, then it is apparent from the foregoing discussion that the exposure time could be based either on measurement of the lowest illumination on the easel — a subject highlight, or on the maximum illumination, which is the area corresponding to the darkest shadow. Theoretically, measurement of either of these areas will give the same result provided that the grade of paper being used exactly suits the negative.

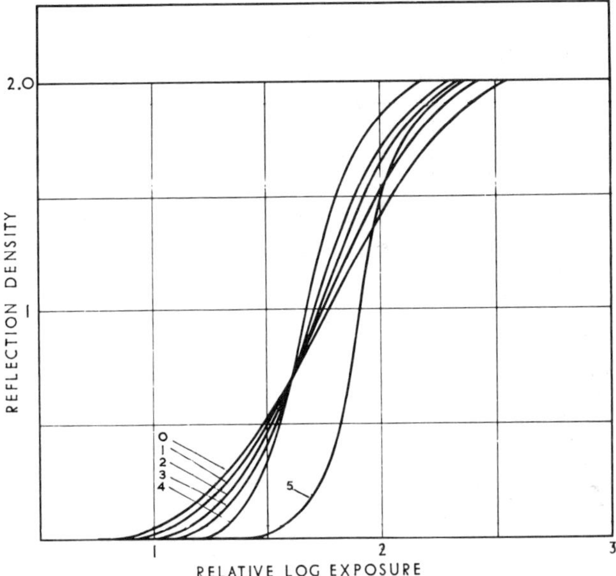

Fig. 1.3 Characteristic curves of six grades of glossy bromide papers showing how exposure range differs from grade to grade. These curves are for Ilfobrom papers.

On-easel photometry involving measurement of the lightest or darkest area in the image on the paper is equivalent to measurement of the D_{min} or D_{max} of the negative using an ordinary densitometer except that on-easel measurement takes into account the degree of enlargement and other factors. The instructions for using a commercial enlarging photometer often contain the recommendation that a highlight tone in which detail is required should be measured rather than say, a white cloud. If the photometer is one that is used for measuring the brightest area of the image on the enlarger easel, it is often stipulated that the darkest subject tone in which gradation is wanted should be chosen.

Neither of the foregoing is equivalent to measuring the effective D_{max} or D_{min} of a negative and the photographer has the problem of choosing the most appropriate area to measure. Ideally, a unique characteristic of a negative should be chosen as a printing exposure criterion and while D_{min} and D_{max} meet this requirement, a "light tone in which detail can be seen" and a "shadow just showing gradation" do not. A little experience is required to use a photometer to the best advantage so that the most suitable area for measurement can be chosen unerringly.

If a negative in the enlarger carrier has a density range of say, 1.3, then the deepest shadow transmits 20-times as much light as the brightest highlight, 20 being the antilogarithm of 1.3. On the face of it, the illumination range on the easel should also be 20 to 1 but there are two complicating factors to take into account. The first concerns the use of a condenser enlarger which always has a certain amount of specularity, giving an image contrast that is higher than the contrast of the negative itself. This difference is produced by the Callier effect and it can be very big indeed in the case of a condenser and point source enlarger. It is usually fairly small with the usual condenser and opal lamp enlarger.

The second complication is that of non-image forming light or flare falling on the easel. Like flare in a camera it has the effect of reducing image contrast. In enlarging it has its greatest effect on the highlights of the image and in the camera the effect is chiefly in the shadows. Flare in an enlarger is usually small in amount as the optical conditions are not quite those of a camera. In the first instance the contrast of a negative is much less than that of the average scene in front of a camera. Secondly, the area of negative being enlarged is, or should be, masked so that no light from outside the field of view of the lens falls on the lens. The lens itself however gives rise to a little non-image forming light even if it is bloomed and free from dust. (Figure 1.4).

These two opposing effects, specularity and flare tend to cancel each other out but the printing contrast of a negative in a condenser enlarger is usually a little higher than its contrast as measured by a densitometer. This influences choice of paper grade for a particular negative more than anything else, and the photographer is well able to make his choice on the basis of the appearance of the image on the easel. Thus a harder grade of paper is required for a particular negative when using a fully-diffused enlarger such as one fitted with a cold-cathode head than with a condenser

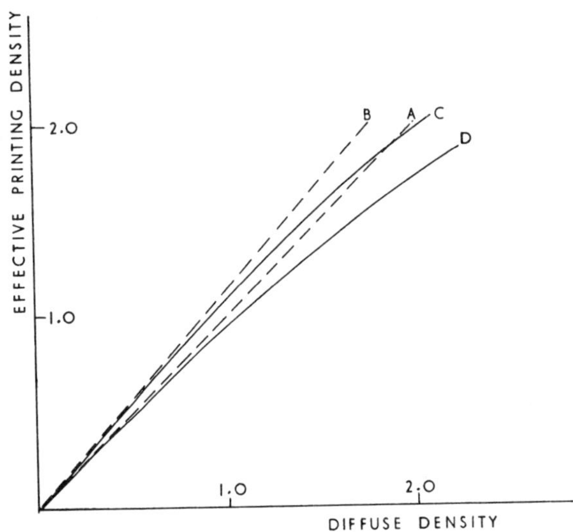

Fig. 1.4 Showing the effects of specularity and flare in an enlarger on the contrast of the image. The broken line A represents contact printing and enlarging with a flare-free diffused light enlarger. Curve B is for a condenser enlarger with no flare. Curve C represents a condenser enlarger having an average amount of flare. Curve D is for a diffuse light enlarger with average flare.

enlarger. Specularity is nil with a fully-diffused enlarger and flare tends to be more than with a condenser enlarger.

If enlarging exposures are determined by measuring a near-highlight on the enlarger baseboard, the effects of any flare and specularity are taken into account automatically. If a shadow is measured, on which neither flare nor specularity have any significant effect, the presence of either or both is dealt with by the choice of the most suitable grade of paper. It must be reiterated that, if the choice of paper grade is correct, measurement of a highlight or a shadow should give the same result.

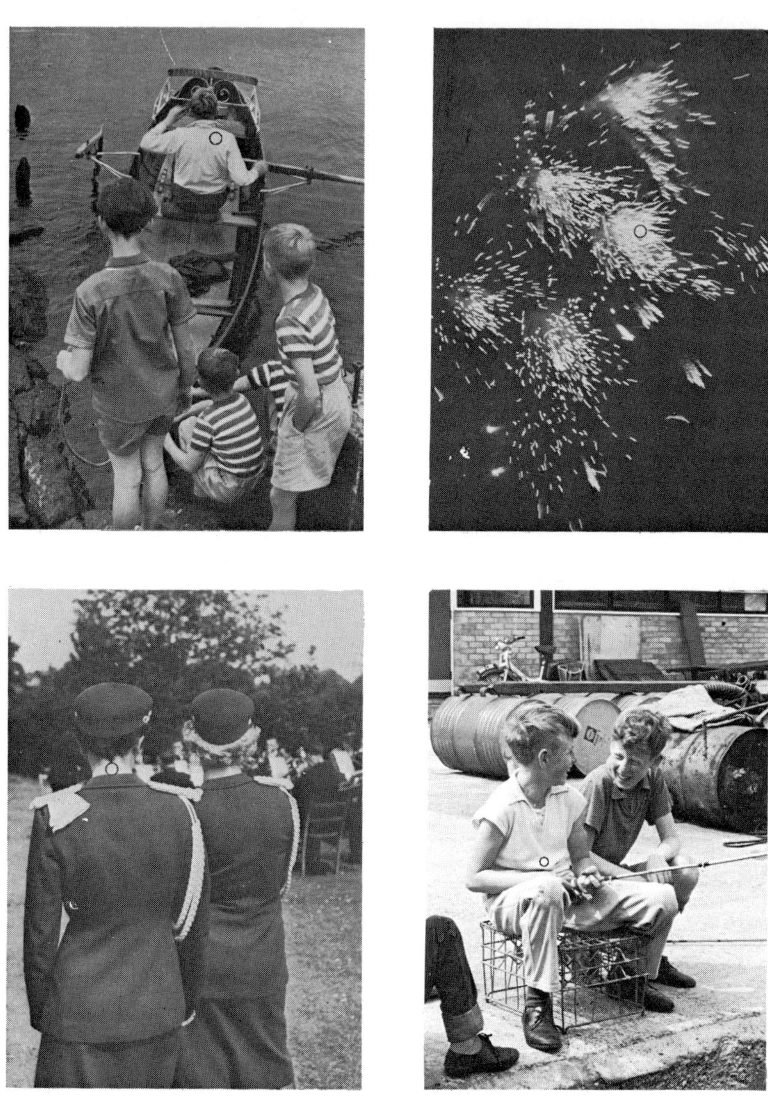

Fig. 1.5 Prints of different subjects exposed with the aid of a spot photometer for measuring a highlight area on the enlarger baseboard.

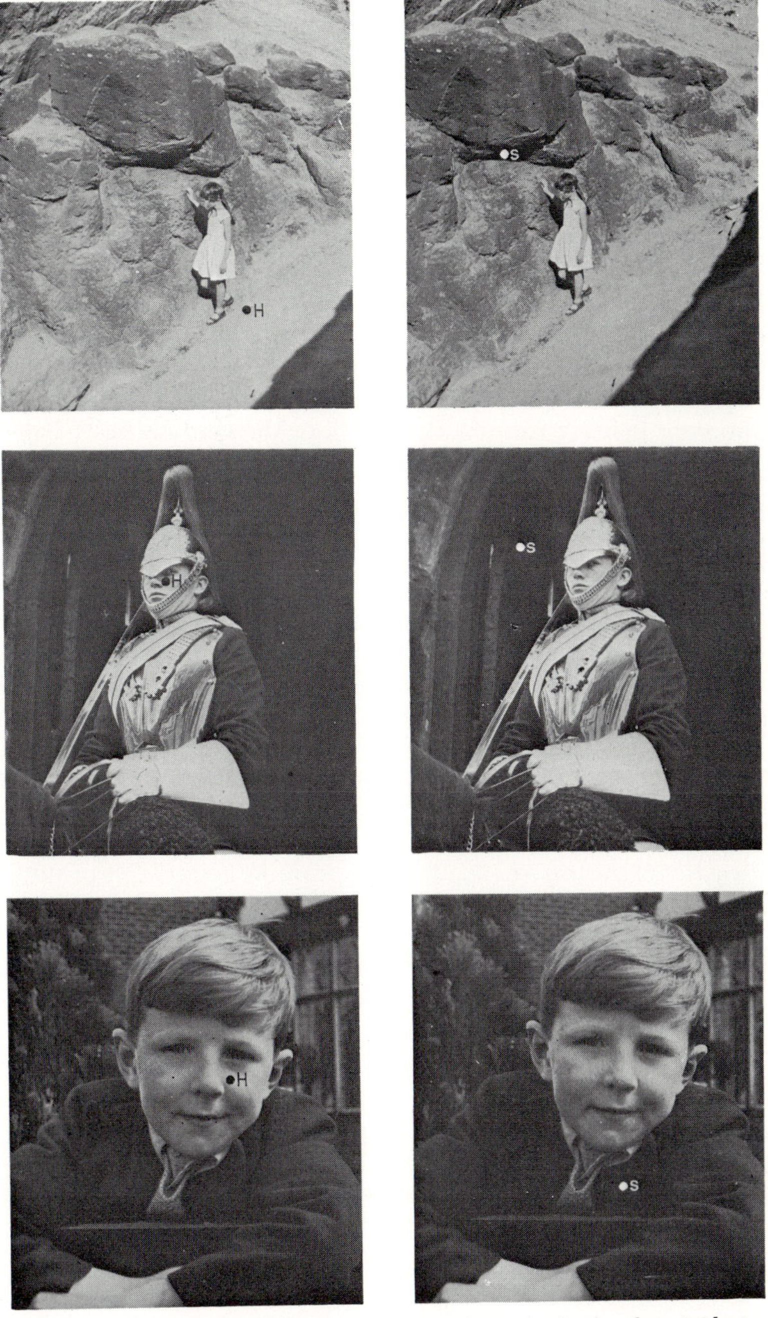

Fig. 1.6 These pairs of prints were exposed on the basis of spot photo-meter measurements on the enlarger easel. One of each pair was exposed for a near-highlight and the other for a shadow in which detail was just visible. Both methods give satisfactory results and the areas measured are indicated by a black spot and a white spot on each print.

In saying that the most suitable grade of paper for a particular negative is one having a log exposure range equal to the density range of the negative, it is more accurate to state that the log exposure range should be equal to the log illumination range of the image falling on the paper. The former statement is correct for contact printing but most prints are made by projection because of the popularity of small format cameras.

It would simplify matters considerably if it could be said that a spot photometer should be used for measuring either the very lightest tone in the image or the very darkest. These can be found beyond doubt merely by looking for the tones that give the largest and smallest readings light-wise. Unfortunately, in pictorial printing, it happens often that a shadow has to be pushed up above the upper limiting point on the paper curve or a highlight right down on the toe so that it prints as perfectly white. With any kind of spot photometer the photographer cannot be absolved from making a choice as to the most suitable tone for measurement on the basis of the subject and the rendering required of it.

As an alternative to spot photometry for the estimation of enlarging exposures, the average illumination on the easel can be evaluated by means of an integrating photometer. This is more or less equivalent to the normal use of a photoelectric exposure meter for determining camera exposures. It is equivalent also to the measurement of the "total density" of the negative which is given the symbol "$\bar{D}$". This type of measurement is employed in automatic rollhead printers used in photofinishing and it is used on colour printers as well.

One advantage of measuring the average illumination on the easel or the $\bar{D}$ of the negative, is that it calls for no selection or judgement on the part of the photographer. Total density is a unique characteristic of a negative and it is worthy of consideration on this account alone. Because the density distributions of negatives are so varying. $\bar{D}$ as a printing exposure criterion might be thought unreliable and likely to lead to errors. This is, in fact, true but the magnitude of such errors is discussed fully in a later chapter along with methods of dealing with them.

It is worth pointing out that a spot photometer can be used for integrated readings merely by covering the enlarger lens with a piece of ground glass or similar diffusing material and measuring this scrambled light on the enlarger easel by placing the photocell immediately below the lens. The total densities of negatives for enlarging can be measured off the easel and the values obtained used for arriving at the correct exposure times. In this case, the magnification and lens aperture have to be taken into account separately but, as the calculations required can be made very simple, this is no great disadvantage.

It can be assumed that the printing exposure required by a negative is inversely proportional to its light transmission. The logarithm of the exposure time is hence directly proportional to the density of the negative. The latter statement is true when it refers to the density of an individual tone such as a highlight or a shadow but it is not necessarily true for total density. It is possible to have two negatives with identical total densities but requiring different printing exposures.

In considering the relative merits of measuring D_{min}, D_{max} or $\bar{D}$ of a negative for the purpose of arriving at a suitable printing exposure, it is as well to take into account the possible effects of using a grade of paper not ideally suited to the negative. Suppose that a spot reading is taken of the darkest or near-darkest area of the image on the easel and this used for estimating exposure. If the negative exactly fits the exposure range of the paper then, automatically, the shadows of the resulting print will be of suitable depth and will have satisfactory gradation. If the paper is too hard for the negative however, the print shadows will be uniformly black and devoid of gradation. Too soft a grade of paper on the other hand will mean grey shadows with no full black anywhere. (Figure 1.7).

The same arguments apply to the use of a spot photometer for measuring the brightest part of the image, corresponding to a shadow. An excessively hard paper will produce snowy-white highlights showing no detail. Too soft a paper will yield grey highlights much too far removed from the white of the paper. (Figure 1.8).

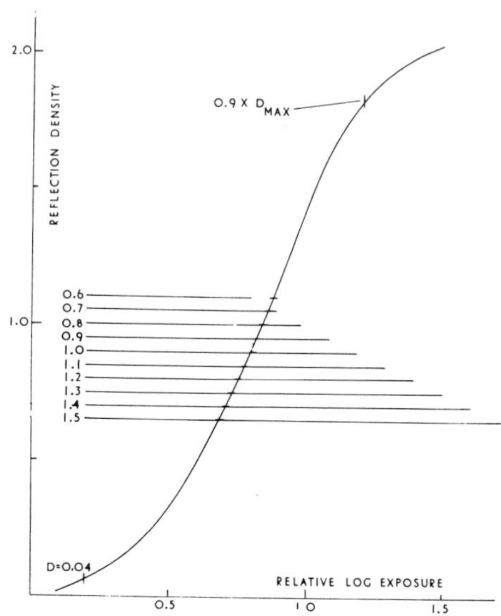

Fig. 1.7 The effect of mismatch of negative and paper grade when using a spot photometer for measuring a highlight in the image on the enlarger easel.

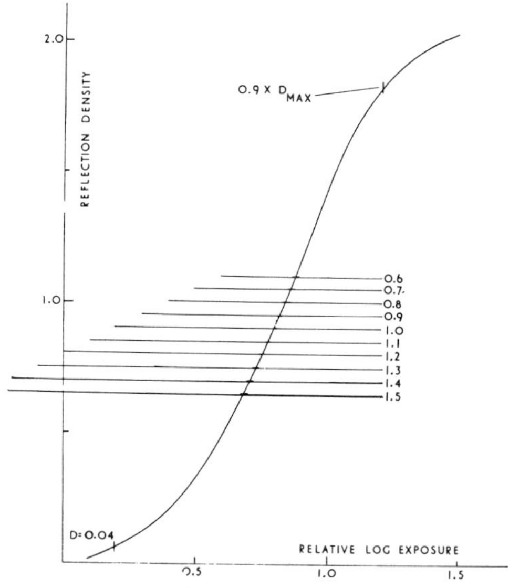

Fig. 1.8 Mismatch of negative and paper grade and the use of a spot photometer for shadow measurement.

A spot photometer can be used for measuring the illumination range of the image on the easel and from this information the most suitable grade of paper can be selected. This is not infallible however as it sometimes happens that the best print from a "difficult" negative is obtained on a harder paper than is indicated by the density range of the negative, using local exposure control in the form of shading and printing-up. A photometer can be used even in this context for working out the exposure modifications required but how far this is an adequate substitute for trial exposures is a matter for the individual to decide.

Integrated measurements of the light falling on the easel or measurement of the $\overline{D}$ of negatives are less affected by an unsuitable choice of paper grade than are spot measurements. Assuming a negative of average density distribution it can be shown that when using $\overline{D}$ as a criterion, exposures are such as to place a more or less mid-tone somewhere in the middle of the characteristic curve of the paper. A good compromise between highlights and shadows is obtained if the paper used is harder or softer than it should be.

In Figure 1.9 is shown the characteristic curve of a hypothetical glossy paper with a log exposure range of 1.0 as

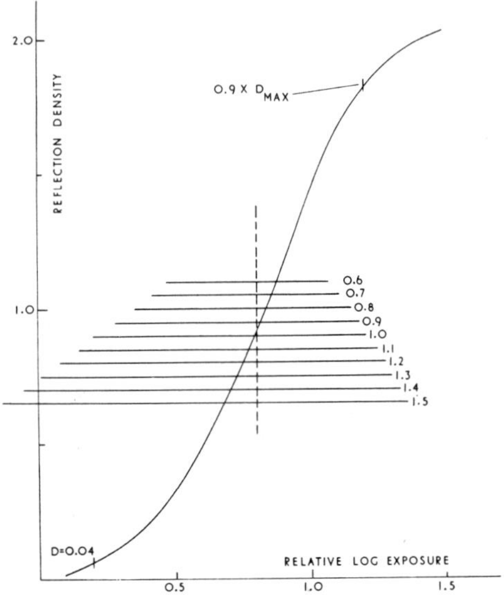

Fig. 1.9 When using an integrating enlarging meter the effects of using the wrong grade of paper are not as severe as with a spot photometer as can be seen by comparing this diagram with Fig. 1.7 and 1.8.

evaluated in accordance with American Standard Ph 2 : 2–
1966. Following this Standard, the $\bar{D}$ of a negative with
even density distribution is located on the paper curve at a
density of about 0.9 above base plus fog density. This in a
print of good quality from the point of view of general
density. On the characteristic curve in Figure 1.9 are shown
the locations of the scales of negatives of higher and lower
contrast than one exactly fitting the exposure range of the
paper. As can be seen, in both cases there is a fairly equal
sacrifice of highlight and shadow quality. The point can be
made therefore that, using $\bar{D}$ as a criterion for estimating
printing exposures, success does not depend too much on the
correct choice of paper grade.

CHAPTER TWO

MEASURABLE CHARACTER-ISTICS OF A NEGATIVE

There are three readily measurable characteristics of a negative that can be used as a basis for estimating printing exposures. These are, minimum density, maximum density and total density. These have already been discussed briefly in the previous chapter. All three have the quality that they are unique. This desirable quality of uniqueness does not extend to "the deepest significant shadow" or to the "darkest tone in the image on the baseboard in which detail is required. It is partly for this reason that many amateurs have found enlarging spot photometers unreliable at times because of the difficulty of selecting the most appropriate tone in every negative.

The minimum and maximum densities of a negative can be measured in the negative itself using a conventional transmission densitometer. The only requirement is that the instrument shall be capable of measuring a small area as in 35 mm negatives in particular, the deepest shadow and brightest highlight may be tiny. An almost equally important requirement is that it must be possible to locate a selected small area of a negative precisely in the light beam. Some transmission densitometers are very deficient in this respect as the makers appear to assume that always a big area of a sample will be measured which presents no difficulty as regards location in the light beam.

The S.E.I. exposure photometer with the associated accessories to adapt it as a densitometer is particularly good as it measures a very small area indeed and this can be located very precisely in the visual field. The S.E.I. is a visual comparator and, as such, it is more tiring to use over long periods than an electronic densitometer.

Total density can be measured with very simple equipment of comparatively low sensitivity. A simple optical bench equipped with a light source, negative stage or carrier, and an exposure meter such as one of the Weston Master series, is perfectly adequate and the sensitivity of such an arrangement can be made high enough for measuring the total densities of small negatives such as 35 mm and half-frame. Alternatively, a suitable selenium or cadmium sulphide photocell and a 50-microampere moving coil meter can be built into a home-made photometer for measuring total density. Several ideas on these lines are offered in a later chapter. (Figure 2.1).

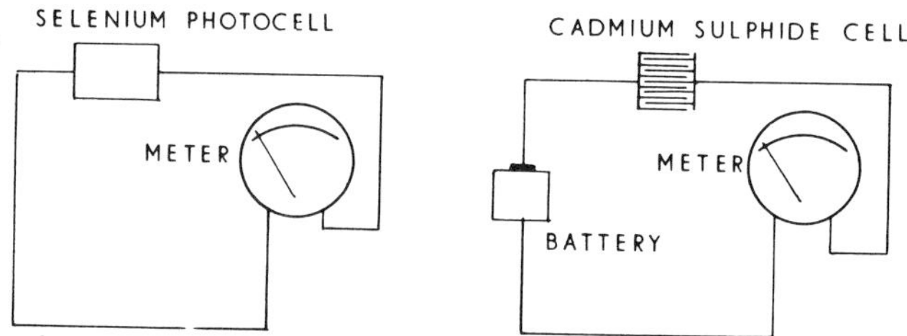

Fig. 2.1 Basic circuits for an enlarging photometer utilising a selenium photocell and a cadmium sulphide photoresistive cell.

Effective minimum, maximum and total densities can be measured on the enlarger baseboard, the first two with a spot photometer and the last with almost any kind of photometer no matter how large or small its photocell, by placing a "scrambler" of matt glass or plastic below the enlarger lens while taking a reading.

There are obvious advantages in measuring on the easel. In the first instance the degree of enlargement and the lens aperture are taken into account, doing away with the need for considering them separately as factors affecting printing exposures. Secondly, the effects of enlarger specularity and lens flare on the illumination in the highlight areas of the image are included in the measurements where such areas are used as a basis for exposure estimation.

There are also disadvantages in on-easel measurement. It is rather time-consuming for obvious reasons and there may be difficulty in reading instrument scales in the dim safe-lighting. As the light sensitor of an enlarging photometer has to be sensitive to low levels of illumination it is affected by the printing safelights. This means either complete screening of the photocell so that it is affected only by light from the enlarger lens or that the safelights have to be switched off while readings are being taken. Several commercially-available enlarging exposure meters include a switch that operates to turn off the safelights while readings are being taken. Without some such arrangement, using a meter is rather frustrating and it adds considerably to the time required for producing a batch of enlargements. This is not a viable proposition for the professional worker as the saving of a few sheets of paper may not offset the extra cost of an operator's time.

CHAPTER THREE

PRINCIPLE OF SPOT PHOTOMETRY

The most popular type of enlarging photometer capable of measuring small areas of the image on the enlarger baseboard consists essentially of a small photocell on the end of a flexible lead, the latter being connected to some kind of electrical measuring instrument. One of the problems is that of achieving more than adequate sensitivity as the area measured has to be small and the illumination on the cell can be very low if a highlight area is being measured.

For this reason, the selenium photocell is virtually useless for the purpose as its current output is too low. The cadmium sulphide photo-resistive cell has the advantage of very high sensitivity and it is the usual choice of makers of non-visual enlarging exposure meters. One method of employing such a cell is in the form of a bridge circuit the cell forming the variable resistance in one side of the bridge and a suitable arrangement of variable resistors forming the other half. The resistance of the cell varies with the illumination falling on it, the more the illumination the lower the resistance. Balance of the bridge is indicated by means of a magic-eye indicator or a centre-zero galvanometer. (Figure 3.1).

In instruments of this type the information given by the photocell circuit may be transferred automatically to an electronic timing circuit so that the correct exposure may be given without reference to any instrument scales or a clock. This is convenient when there is no shading or printing-up involved but when there is, it is desirable to be able to watch the passage of the exposure on a conventional timer so that the local control can be applied at the right moments.

An alternative scheme is to have a simple cell and meter circuit with which the illumination in the image area being measured controls the needle deflection of the meter. The scale of the latter can be calibrated in any suitable manner for the calculation of the correct exposure times. This has to

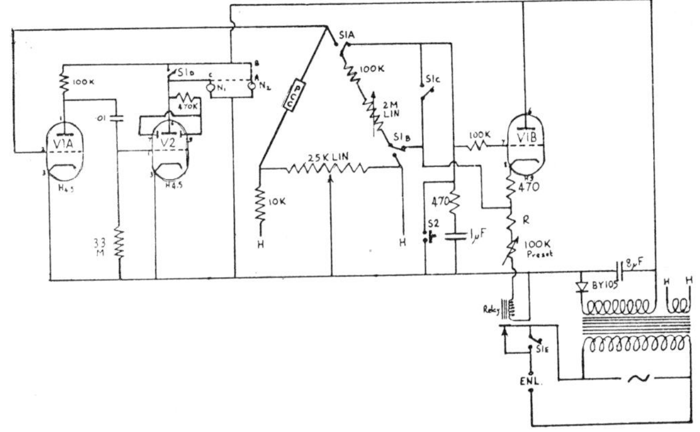

Fig. 3.1 The theoretical circuit of the "Melico" enlarging meter/timer.

be done in such a way that the various speeds of the different papers in use can be taken into account.

The CdS cell has certain undesirable characteristics. It responds rather slowly to changes in the level of illumination especially at low light intensities. This is to the extent that it may be recommended that the operator waits for some seconds before taking the reading after locating the cell in the area to be measured. At very low light levels it may take as long as 30 seconds for the resistance of the cell to reach a stable value. When a CdS cell has been stored in darkness for a period it is necessary to expose it to light for a few minutes in order to restore its normal working characteristics.

The spectral sensitivity of the photocell of an enlarging photometer is of some importance. Although the usual enlarger illuminant, at least as far as the amateur is concerned, is a tungsten filament lamp, ordinary printing papers are sensitive to violet, blue and perhaps to blue-green light. The spectral sensitivity curve of a CdS cell drops very sharply in the blue region of the spectrum and may reach zero at about 450 millimicrons. On the other hand, such cells are highly sensitive to red and infra-red, regions of the spectrum to which printing papers are completely unresponsive. (Figure 3.2).

This difference between the spectral sensitivity of the photocell and that of the printing paper is of little importance

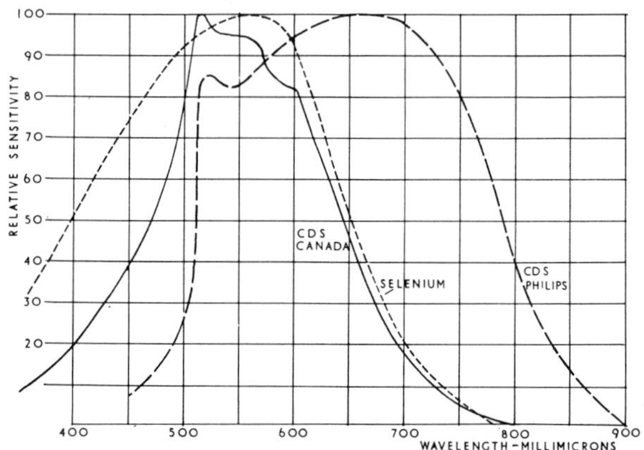

Fig. 3.2 The spectral sensitivities of selenium and cadmium sulphide photocells. The two curves for the CdS cell are those from the Philips Laboratories (broken line) and from National Semiconductors Ltd., Canada (solid line).

provided that the colour temperature of the printing source remains constant and that the silver deposits of negatives are always substantially neutral in colour. If the colour temperature of the enlarging source falls, making the light relatively richer in red and infra-red, it will make little difference to the CdS cell which is so highly sensitive in these regions. It is likely to make a big difference to the printing exposures required as the paper reacts mainly to blue light.

If a set of negatives has slightly brownish images due to the use of a very fine-grain developer or one that stains somewhat, the densities to blue light will be higher than those of similar negatives having neutral images. Again, a CdS meter will be largely unaffected because of the very small contribution made by blue light to the measurements. The printing exposures needed will, however, be much longer than usual. Fortunately, the colour temperature of a tungsten light source does not change suddenly although it drops slowly with ageing. Equally fortunately, modern developers do not stain and they do not produce warm-tone silver images as did some fine-grain formulae of years ago incorporating para-phenylene diamine.

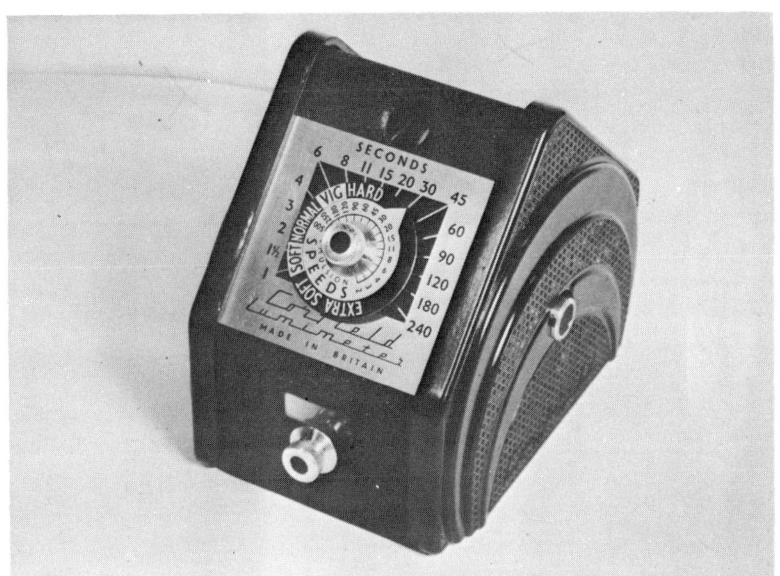

Fig. 3.3 The Corfield "Lumimeter", an inexpensive visual spot photometer.

It is as well to realise that a CdS enlarging photometer adjusted to indicate correct exposures when used with a particular enlarger, may require adjustment to the general level of the indicated exposures when moving it to another enlarger. This will certainly be the case in changing from a tungsten enlarger to one fitted with a cold cathode fluorescent source or the other way round.

There have been several visual enlarging photometers of which the Corfield "Lumimeter" is well-known. Although Corfield Ltd. went out of business some years ago, the "Lumimeter" is still being made and is distributed by the Rank Organisation. It is much less expensive than an electronic photometer but it gives reliable results. It is based on the Bunsen greasespot principle and a light source of continuously variable intensity is compared visually with the illumination in a selected tone in the image on the enlarger easel, the two parts of the visual field being brought to equality by rotation of a knob. A dial attached to the knob carries a scale of exposure times and the appropriate one is read off. Provision is made for the use of papers of different speeds. (Figure 3.4).

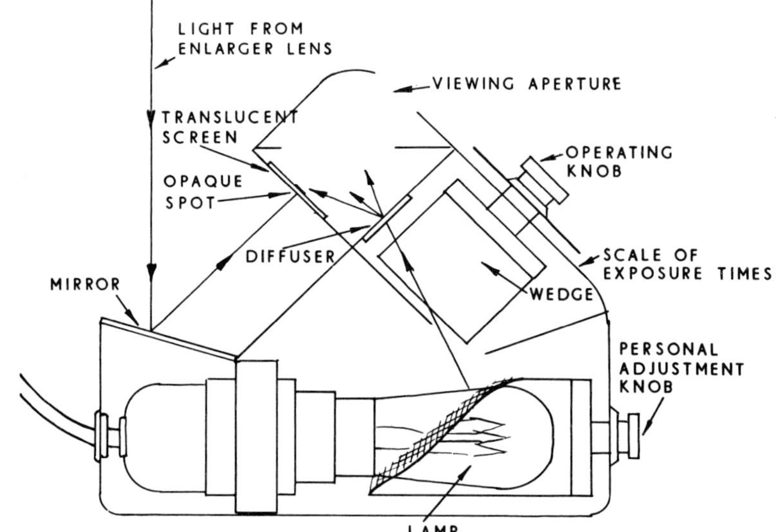

Fig. 3.4 Sectional view of the Corfield "Lumimeter".

Although the human eye is a very poor judge of absolute light intensities it is very sensitive to even small differences in the brightness of small contiguous areas and such a visual photometer can be a very effective device for on-easel estimation of enlarging exposures. The S.E.I. exposure photometer can be used for the same purpose although it assesses illumination indirectly by measuring the luminance of a selected tone on the enlarger easel, the latter being covered with a sheet of clean white paper. The small numbers on the scales of the S.E.I. are difficult to read under safelight conditions and there is some difficulty in holding the instrument steady while measuring a small area. As it is a visual instrument, changes in the colour temperature of the exposing light will not alter the level of the indicated exposures. Ideally, any measuring device should have the same spectral response as the sensitive material for which exposures are being determined.

A spot photometer for enlarging should be capable of measuring a relatively small area — a circle $\frac{1}{8}$ in. in diameter is not too small. With a visual instrument this presents no difficulty but with one utilising a photocell, the smaller the area being measured, the smaller the light energy involved and the higher the sensitivity needed. In the absence of adequate sensitivity it may be found necessary to measure the selected area of the image with the enlarger lens at full aperture and then to stop down to the aperture it is proposed to use for making the exposure, working out the increase required on the basis of the extent of stopping down.

In following the last procedure one has to guard against error arising from an anomalous series of f/numbers on a particular lens. It is not uncommon to encounter a series thus — f/4.5, f/5.6, f/8, f/11 and so forth. This is an ill-considered series in that the exposure interval between f/4.5 and f/5.6 is not the usual factor of 2; it is only about $1\frac{1}{2}$. Some enlarging lenses do not have f/numbers but numbers such as 1, 2, 4, 8, and 16. These represent exposure factors assuming that the exposure is worked out for open aperture. It should not be assumed that the click stops on an enlarging lens are accurate. The "clicks" may not be in the right places and this gives rise to irregularities as the lens is stopped down. This is an easy thing to check and if errors are found, allowances can be made for them if they are big enough to be significant.

It has become apparent recently that the spectral response of a CdS photocell is debatable. Curves published by the Philips research laboratories show a spectral response as described previously. Curves published by a Canadian manufacturer however show a spectral sensitivity closely akin to that of the human eye when adapted to normal levels of illumination. The CdS cells normally encountered certainly have most sensitivity in the red and infra-red and relatively little in the blue region.

CHAPTER FOUR

COMMERCIAL ENLARGING SPOT PHOTOMETERS

It can be dangerous for an author to describe specialised instruments in a book as they are liable to minor and even drastic changes so that descriptions are out-of-date even before the book is published. It is always advisable to consult a photographic dealer regarding available equipment to be certain of securing the latest information and to learn if new models have appeared and old ones discontinued. Despite changes, the basic principles of photometry do not alter and this is sufficient justification for discussing currently available instruments.

The "Melico" enlarging exposure meter/timer is available in several models. It is made by Medical and Electrical Instrumentation Ltd, 32–34 Gordon House Rd, London N.W.5. It consists of a CdS spot photometer with which is incorporated an electronic time switch circuit. It thus not only determines the required exposure times but sets them up automatically on the timer. The meter is provided with a supply socket to provide the enlarger lamp with current and it has a cable for plugging into the mains supply. The instrument is double insulated and is fitted with twin cables. When it is in use it is advisable to earth the enlarger column and lamphouse by means of a suitable wire connected to the nearest main water pipe provided that this is known to be an effective earth.

The small CdS cell is contained in a metal housing on a length of thin cable. A metal mask over the cell confines the effective area to a circle $\frac{1}{8}$ in. in diameter which means that a very small area of the image can be measured. The colour model of the "Melico" has provision for covering the cell with each of a set of tricolour filters in turn for the determination of exposure times and filter packs in colour printing.

The control panel of the instrument (Figure 4.2) is laid out conveniently and it carries two switches. A "press-on, press-off" switch labelled, "function", brings the photo-

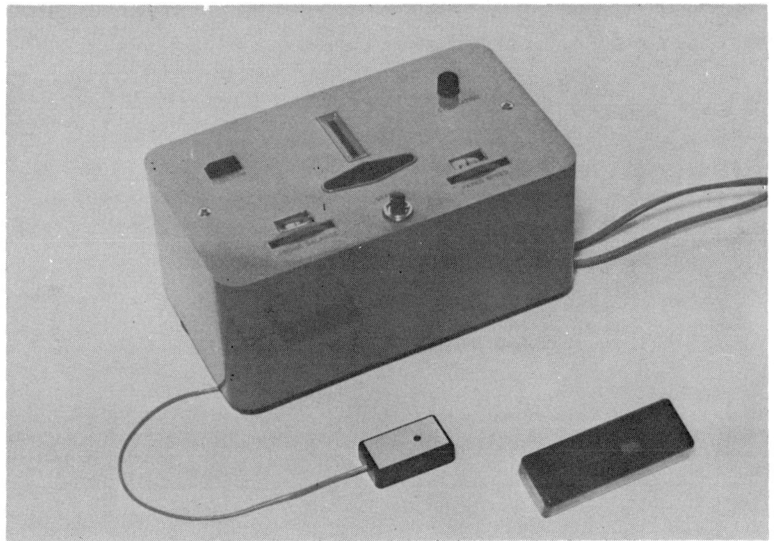

Fig. 4.1 The "Melico" enlarging meter (colour model). The CdS photo-cell probe can be seen.

on the enlarger lamp. The switch is depressed after taking a reading to turn off the enlarger lamp in readiness for making an exposure. The second switch is the "start" button for the timer and it has to be pressed and immediately released as the time for which it is held depressed is added to the exposure time given by the timer.

A calibrated control numbered 0.1 to 10 is for setting up the speed of the paper in use. These numbers are purely arbitrary and they are not related in any way to any accepted system of paper speed numbers. Furthermore, the higher the number on the scale the slower the paper which is a wholly illogical arrangement and one that could have easily been avoided. A similar calibrated control labelled "probe balance" is used in conjunction with the photocell to produce the widest possible separation between the illuminated strips of the magic eye indicator. When this has been done the electronic timer has been set to give the correct exposure time. The probe balance scale is numbered from 1 to 20 and these are relative exposure times. This range is rather small in practical

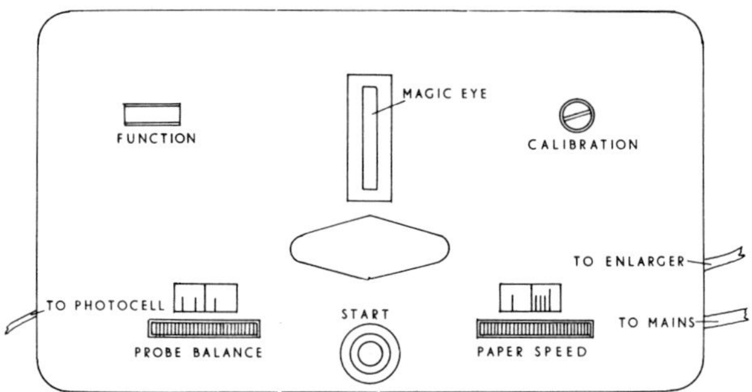

Fig. 4.2 Showing the arrangement of the control panel of the "Melico" enlarging meter.

use and it is often necessary to take a reading with the lens at full aperture and, on stopping down to say two stops, to operate the timer four times. This becomes necessary when making big enlargements from dense negatives.

There is a calibration control on the panel the purpose of which is to set the general level of exposure times to suit the enlarging conditions and preferences of the photographer. It works by altering the durations of the exposures for the various positions of the probe balance. For example, with the calibration control turned fully counter-clockwise, the numbers on the probe balance scale denote times in seconds. Thus, the range of the timer is now from 1 to 20 seconds. If the calibration control is rotated fully clockwise, all the times are increased by a factor of 3 and the range is now from 3 to 60 seconds. Intermediate positions of the control give intermediate ranges of exposure times.

When once the calibration control has been set to suit particular working conditions it does not have to be altered until the conditions are changed. It is a simple matter to draw up a chart showing actual exposure times in seconds for the various numbers on the probe balance scale for any setting of the calibration knob. Such a chart has to be drawn up every time the calibration has to be altered for any reason. It is worth drawing attention to the fact that while alteration of the calibration changes the duration of the exposures, the paper speed control does not. It simply changes the probe balance position for a particular light intensity on the cell. (Figure 4.3).

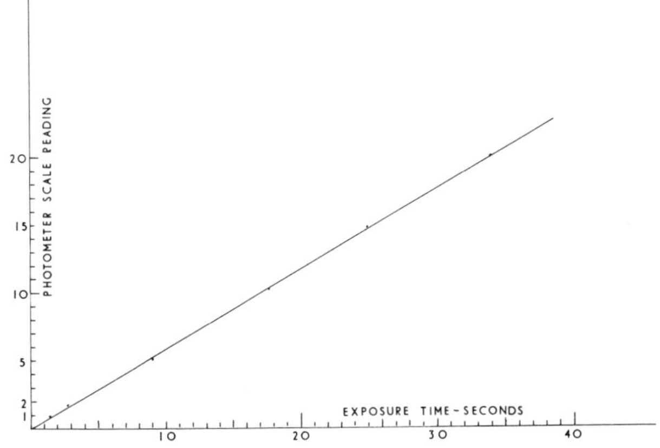

Fig. 4.3 A typical calibration chart for the "Melico" enlarging meter. Exposure times in seconds are plotted against the probe balance control readings.

The procedure for using the "Melico" is to switch it on and set the function switch in the up position. A few minutes should be allowed as a warming-up period for the best accuracy. The probe is now placed on the enlarger baseboard and the cell located in the area it is proposed to measure. The mask over the cell is white to make for good visibility of the image. Checking that the paper speed is correctly set, the probe balance is rotated until the shadow gap in the magic eye is at its widest.

The function switch is now pressed to the down position to turn off the enlarger lamp and the magic eye. The safe-lights, which have to be off while measurements are being made, are now switched on and the paper exposed by pressing the start button and releasing it.

The makers suggest that the forehead or cheek in a portrait are suitable areas to measure. In a landscape the sky is better avoided and a detail chosen that is required to print as a light grey. These recommendations mean that the absolute D_{max} of a negative is avoided and we are faced with the situation that a unique characteristic of the negative is not being measured. The user is therefore called upon to be discriminating and this calls for some experience if consistent results are to be obtained.

The "Melico", like any other spot photometer, can be used for measuring the integrated light on the baseboard which is equivalent to measuring the effective total density of the negative. A piece of ground glass or matt plastic is placed in front of the enlarger lens while a measurement is being made. It is stated by the makers that, while this method obviates the need for selecting the most suitable highlight, it is not as accurate as the spot reading system. This is arguable and many workers, in fact, find integrated readings more reliable than spot readings from near-highlights.

There is no reason, of course, why any spot photometer should not be used for measuring the brightest part of the image on the easel. This is equivalent to measuring the minimum density of the negative. It may be considered preferable to measure the darkest shadow in which detail is required in the enlargement. In this case the measurement is not strictly of the minimum negative density but, in most cases, it will be close to it. There is always likely to be some doubt on this point; in many pictorial shots the very extreme shadows have no important detail in them and are allowed to print as the full black of the paper.

If the brightest area of the image is measured instead of the darkest or near-darkest as may be recommended by the makers of the photometer being used, the paper speed setting will have to be modified to suit the changed method of use. The brightest part of the image will give a much smaller indicated exposure than the darkest and hence the paper speed setting has to be for a much slower speed to bring indicated exposures back to their correct values.

The "Melico" has proved a very satisfactory instrument in use despite the criticisms levelled at it previously. It is rather strange that, very often, electronic instruments designed for photographic purposes are excellent as regards their circuitry and electrical design but somewhat deficient photographically.

The Philips automatic timers, of which there are two models at the time of writing, are similar to the "Melico" in many ways and their features are such that it appears the

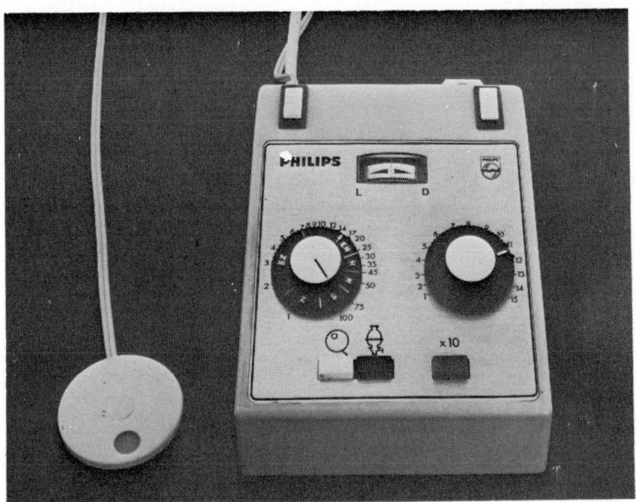

Fig. 4.4 The Philips automatic time PDT 021.

designer tried to avoid the minor faults found in the "Melico". Unfortunately, this has not been done with complete success as will be shown later. The PDT 021 model is the more elaborate and sensitive of the two versions and the range of exposures covered is from 0.5 to 150 seconds — 1 to 300 which is fully adequate. The circuitry is completely solid-state as against the valve circuitry of the "Melico".

The Philips auto timer PDT 021 has a CdS probe on the end of a flexible cable and this is connected to the control box. The panel carries five press switches, two knobs and a balance indicator. The latter is a precise measuring instrument with a moving needle and balance is shown by the needle resting centrally on the scale. An on-off switch brings the instrument into use as required and by depressing the left-hand button of a pair of switches the enlarger lamp is switched on and the safelights in the room switched off. Two sockets at the rear of the control box provide connections for the enlarger and safelights. With the paper speed setting adjusted for the paper in use, a near-highlight tone is measured on the enlarger easel by rotating the time control knob until the indicator needle is centred. A push switch marked "X 10" is depressed should the time control knob have to be rotated fully clockwise without reaching the balance point. (Figure 4.5).

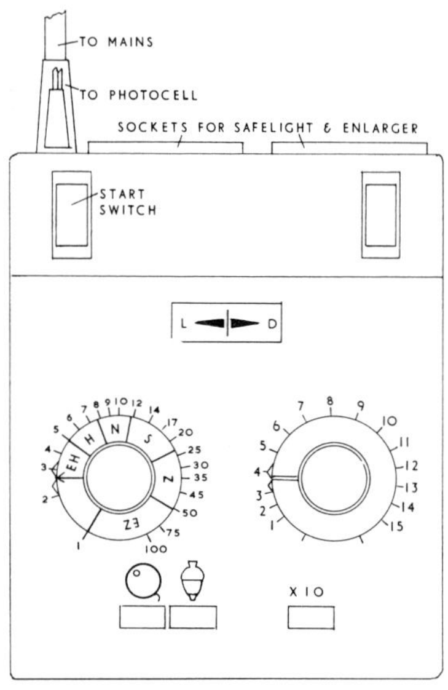

Fig. 4.5 The control panel of the Philips automatic timer model PDT 021.

The right-hand button of the pair of switches is now pressed to switch off the enlarger lamp and to switch on the safelights. The timing circuit has been automatically set to the correct exposure time by the balancing operation and, with the printing paper in position on the baseboard, the "start" is depressed to initiate the exposure.

There is a built-in "character" control to which access is obtained through a small circular aperture in the side of the control box. This is operated by means of a screwdriver to set the general level of exposure times to suit the equipment in use. The character control alters the balance point for a given level of illumination on the photocell and its range is about 3 to 1 in terms of the exposure time given for a given image brightness.

Provision is made for the determination of the most suitable grade of printing paper. This is carried out by making an additional measurement, this time of the lightest area of the image, and from the highlight and shadow readings the appropriate grade of paper is indicated on a dial. At the same time, the paper speed is set so that the exposure is corrected automatically for the different speeds of different grades of paper.

The paper speed dial on the Philips timers is calibrated on the assumption that the harder the paper grade the slower the paper. This is by no means always true although it will be so for a set of papers having equal middle-tone speeds for all grades. "Ilfobrom" is an example and, with these, five of the six grades have equal speeds for a density of 0.7 and the hardest grade of all is half the speed of the rest. The highlight speeds of some papers are quite irregular from grade to grade and with these the automatic speed adjustment of the Philips timers is of little value. This would not be very important as the user could easily determine the highlight speeds of his favourite papers and set these up manually on the paper sensitivity control. Unfortunately, the range provided by this is only about 2 to 1 which is wholly inadequate to cover all the papers on the market.

Another feature of the Philips timers which makes them open to adverse criticism is that alteration of the paper speed setting changes the actual durations of the exposure for a given balance point. Thus, the numbers on the time control dial indicate seconds when the paper sensitivity is adjusted for a paper of lowest speed. For the fastest paper speed setting the numbers on the time control dial are approximately half-seconds. The user does not know therefore, what actual exposure time is being given in seconds, unless he goes to the trouble to make a calibration chart for every paper speed setting. This does not matter in straight printing but it is a severe handicap when local exposure control is required in the form of "dodging". Most negatives give of their best only with at least a little dodging.

A tolerably simple method of overcoming such a limitation is to forego the use of the paper sensitivity control and to use a series of small neutral density filters to slide over the CdS cell. If the character control is adjusted to give satisfactory prints with the fastest paper in use when readings are taken with no N.D. filter over the cell, then all other papers can be dealt with by placing an appropriate filter over the cell window. For example, for a paper having half the highlight speed of the fastest, an N.D. filter value 0.3 over the cell will reduce the light reaching it by 50-per cent and the indicated exposure will be doubled. Given a big enough range of filters, papers of almost any speed can be used with little difficulty. Such an expedient is somewhat cumbersome and it is pity that the makers did not consider this point more carefully.

The basic soundness of an enlarging spot photometer can be tested very easily. A step-wedge such as one of the Kodak photographic step-tablets should be placed in the negative carrier of the enlarger and focussed to any convenient size. The No. 1 step-tablet is probably the most convenient as it is small enough to go in a miniature enlarger. It is helpful to number the steps of the wedge so that they can be identified in the test prints.

The photometer should be used to measure any step near the minimum density of the wedge and the magnification, f/number, and, if necessary the calibration control on the photometer are adjusted so that the indicated exposure is such as to give a medium density for the selected step on a hard grade of paper as nearly as possible at the shortest time the photometer can indicate. Thus, if a particular photometer can indicate a shortest exposure of $\frac{1}{2}$ second, everything should be adjusted so that this time produces a medium tone on the hard grade of paper in use. This preliminary carried out, all that remains is to expose a number of strips of paper to other steps of the wedge, using the photometer to determine the exposure times. This should be done so that the whole range of times the photometer can indicate is embraced. This may mean increasing the degree of enlargement and stopping down the enlarger lens bearing in mind that the Philips PDT 021 timer can measure such low light levels as call for an exposure time of 150 seconds.

All the strips of paper should be developed together for the same length of time and they should be developed fully to make sure the action has gone nearly to finality. After fixing, washing and drying the densities of the several strips are compared by laying them side by side. Ideally, all the strips should be identical and in this respect, both the "Melico"

Fig. 4.6 Linearity test of "Melico" enlarging computer carried out as described in the text. There are seven different exposure times covering a range of 1 to 20.

Fig. 4.7 A similar test for the Philips automatic timer PDT 021. The eight strips cover a range of exposures of about 1 to 300, a very large range indeed.

and the Philips timers acquit themselves very well indeed. The results of such tests for these two instruments are reproduced in Figures 4.6 and 4.7.

An interesting situation arises with regard to low-intensity reciprocity failure of bromide papers. It can be shown that the magnitude of this is quite substantial at exposure times longer than 30 seconds or so. For example, a particular normal paper was found to require 80 seconds exposure

Fig. 4.8 These patches show typical low-intensity reciprocity of two normal bromide papers. The left-hand patch was exposed for 5 seconds in each case and the middle patches for 50 seconds, the light intensity having been reduced by a factor of 10. The right-hand patches were both given 80 seconds exposure and they match the left-hand patches fairly closely.

where the indicated exposure on the basis of accurate light measurement was 50 seconds. In view of the results obtained with the "Melico" and Philips timers, it must be concluded that correction for low-intensity reciprocity failure has been incorporated in the circuitry and, in fact, this is stated to be the case with the "Melico".

CHAPTER FIVE

HOME-MADE ENLARGING SPOT PHOTOMETERS

The ready availability of both selenium and cadmium sulphide photocells and their low cost present the photographer with ample opportunity for experiment in the field of enlarging photometry. Although the use of a selenium cell is restricted to integrating photometers, the CdS cell is sufficiently sensitive for the measurement of small areas of the image on the enlarger easel.

The cadmium sulphide photoconductive cell consists of a layer of sintered cadmium sulphide on which is deposited metal electrodes that interlace rather like two intermeshed forks. These provide a conducting path in the gap. Gold may be used for the electrodes because of its stability but for the sake of an ohmic junction between the cadmium sulphide and the electrodes, indium or tin is often employed. The CdS cell may be sealed in a glass envelope with dry air making it look rather like a small radio valve or it may be completely encapsulated in transparent plastic. Such cells can be made very small and the area of the sensitive surface may be less than $\frac{1}{4}$ in. across.

When light falls on the cadmium sulphide, electrons are freed within the film, greatly lowering its electrical resistance. The dark resistance of a cell may be, for example, 40 megohms or higher but with an illumination of 100 foot-candles the resistance may drop to about 700 ohms. The cell does not, however, generate current as does a selenium cell and it has to be provided with an external source of supply. A small mercury battery with a nominal voltage of 1.3 volts is often used because this type of battery maintains a very constant voltage until it nears the end of its useful life.

The response of a CdS cell can be made linear over quite a long range and a cell that is linear for a range of illuminations from 0.01 to 1,000 foot-candles is by no means unusual. If a small departure from linearity can be tolerated, extremely

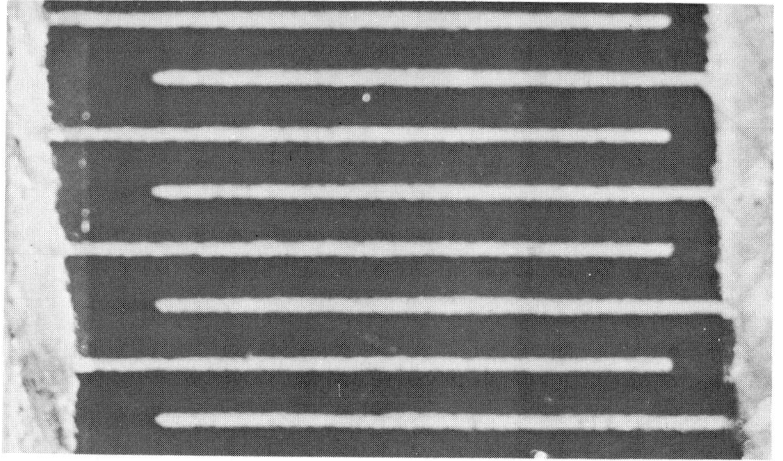

Fig. 5.1 Photomicrograph of a small CdS photocell showing the interlacing electrodes.

high sensitivity is possible which makes this type of cell useful for an enlarging photometer. (Figure 5.2).

The spectral sensitivity of the CdS cell is only very approximately the same as that of the eye and it extends into the deep red and infra-red. In fact, the major part of the sensitivity of a CdS cell lies in the longer wavelengths of the spectrum and beyond. The sensitivity drops sharply in the blue region and sometimes reaches zero at about 450 millimicrons. This lack of agreement between the spectral sensitivity of the cell and that of photographic materials gives rise to difficulties only when there are changes in the colour temperature of the light falling on the cell. In enlarging photometry this is likely to happen only rarely.

A good CdS cell designed expressly for photometry does not show appreciable fatigue. A feature of many such cells is that they become more sensitive during long periods of storage in the dark, but this can be reduced to a very small amount and corrects itself when the cell has been exposed to light for a few minutes.

CdS cells are available in a wide variety of types and sizes. Philips Electrical Ltd. and Mullard Ltd. make them

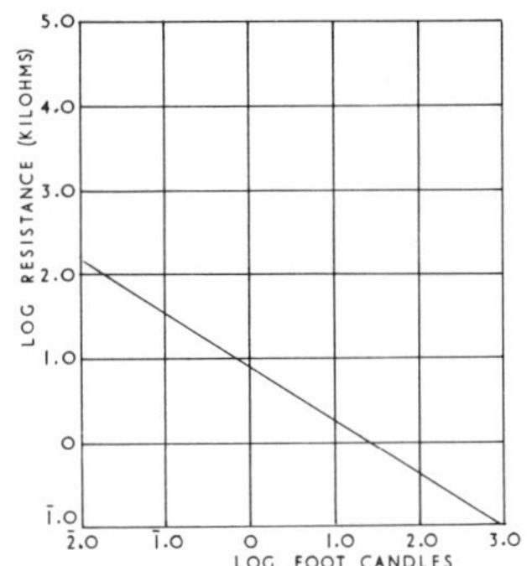

Fig. 5.2 The resistance of a typical cadmium sulphide cell plotted against illumination in foot-candles.

and Hird-Brown Ltd. of Flash Street, Bolton, Lancs list a very wide range of cells made in Canada. The main requirements in a cell for a selective photometer are small size and high sensitivity and these should be coupled with reasonable linearity over a range of at least 1,000 to 1.

It was possible to obtain small cells from a shop selling electronic components. These were such as are used in television receivers for automatic brightness control. The price of CdS cells varies from a few shillings to fifty shillings or more, the higher-priced cells being made to closer tolerances than the cheaper ones.

It is a simple matter to arrive at a rough idea of the sensitivity required in an enlarging photometer. This has just been done for a typical amateur enlarger fitted with a condenser and a 150-watt enlarger lamp and a 3 in. f/4.5 lens. With no negative in the carrier the enlarger was focussed with the lens 20 in. from the baseboard, and with all the room lights turned off the brightness of a sheet of white blotting paper on the easel was measured with a Weston meter, the lens being opened to full aperture.

A reading of 0.4 candles per square foot was obtained, which is equivalent to approximately 1.2 foot-lamberts — the meter reading being multiplied by pi. The latter was rounded off to 3 as only an approximate measurement is needed. A luminance of 1.2 foot-lamberts means an illumination of 1.2 foot-candles, assuming that the white blotting paper

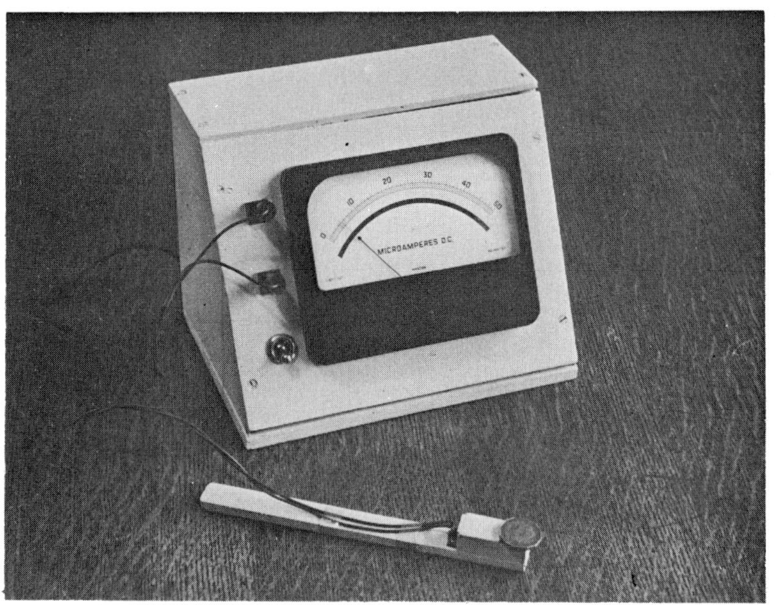

Fig. 5.3 Home-made spot photometer utilising a small CdS cell mounted at one end of a thin strip of wood and enclosed in a plywood housing. The high sensitivity is shown by the needle deflection obtained with the cell amost completely covered with a coin.

has a reflectance of 100 per cent. Multiplying foot-candles by 10 brings them roughly to metre-candles or lux, the unit of illumination used in photographic sensitometry. This gives a figure of 12 lux as the baseboard illumination under the conditions described.

It was calculated from this that with the enlarger lens at 40 in. instead of 20 in. and the lens stopped down to f/22 the illumination would be about 1/10 lux with no negative in the enlarger. For a negative with dense shadows, say, 0.6, the illumination would be reduced to 1/40 lux.

Ideally, therefore, a photometer is required that will measure accurately illumination as low as this.

In practice, less sensitivity could be tolerated, bearing in mind that under such conditions a fast bromide paper would require about 200 seconds exposure. When the enlarger is at the top of its column it is rare that the lens will be stopped

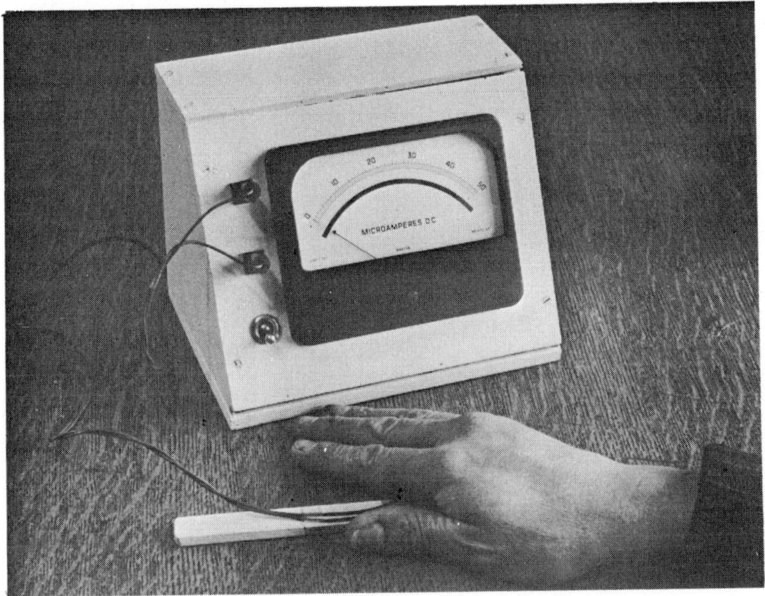

Fig. 5.4 Home-made CdS spot photometer with cell completely shielded from the light. As can be seen from the position of the meter needle the dark current passed by the cell is negligibly small.

right down and, in any case, determination of the exposure could be carried out at a larger aperture, and the time required at the smallest aperture worked out.

The makers' data for CdS cells give a great deal of useful information, including something about sensitivity. This may take the form of a statement regarding the range of illuminations through which a particular cell may be used. For example, a small cell recommended for use in photometry may be suitable for use within the range 0.01 to 1,000 foot-candles, which is equivalent to 0.1 to 10,000 lux.

It will be appreciated that for such applications as in an enlarging photometer, a small sensitive area is required in a cell so that small areas in the image on the baseboard may be measured. A sensitive area less than $\frac{1}{4}$ in. across is quite commonplace, and such a small cell can be extremely sensitive. In the case of a cell $\frac{1}{4}$ or $\frac{3}{8}$ in. across there is no objection to masking it to a circle $\frac{1}{8}$ in. diameter for the sake of being able to measure really small tones. There will be some reduction in sensitivity but this is unlikely to be sufficient to be troublesome.

A microammeter will be required for measuring the current passed by the cell, and a range of 0—50 microamps appears to be convenient. A new meter may cost in the region of five pounds, but a suitable instrument may be found in shops selling government surplus equipment. It is often possible to buy something quite cheaply, but it may

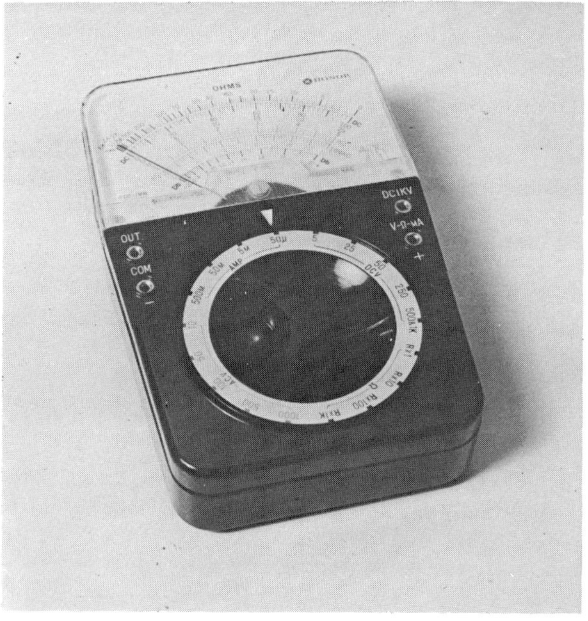

Fig. 5.5 An inexpensive Japanese multi-range test meter which includes a 0 to 50 microampere scale. Such an instrument can be used in an enlarging exposure meter without detriment to its use as a test meter.

not be scaled in microamperes. The author has a moving-coil instrument calibrated in "thousands of yards", but it is essentially a microammeter on the dial of which, nearly out of sight, it is stated that full-scale deflection is equal to 1 milliamp or 1,000 microamps. Yet another such instrument, scaled in numbers from 0 to 100 without any units being stated, has an F.S.D. of 50 microamps.

There are inexpensive multi-range electrical testing instruments on the market and made in Japan and many of these include a 0 to 50 microampere range. The cost is likely to be considerably less than a microammeter on its own and such an item of equipment is useful for all kinds of purposes. Its use as part of a photometer does not preclude its use for other purposes.

It is perhaps better to have an instrument with too small a range than one which is too big, as a small range can be extended by means of shunts connected across the instrument. For example, using a 0–50 microammeter with a coil resistance of 950 ohms, a shunt resistance of one-ninth the coil resistance — 100 ohms is near enough — the reading for any given current flow is reduced by a factor of 10 and the range of 0–50 is extended to 0–500.

By employing a suitable shunt, having a push-to-open switch to disconnect it as required, the range of a photometer may be greatly extended. At high levels of illumination the shunt is used, and at low levels, when needle deflections become small, the shunt is disconnected. With the shunt in circuit all scale readings have to be multiplied by 10; when no shunt is used the readings are taken as they are on the scale. The movement of the meter needle becomes a little sluggish when the shunt is in circuit; the lower the resistance the greater the damping effect.

A cadmium sulphide cell can be used with quite a wide range of voltages, but a low voltage should be used with a small cell as a rule. The 1.3 volts supplied by a mercury cell is usually adequate and the effect of increasing the voltage is merely to increase the needle deflection for a given level of illumination on the CdS cell. The relationship follows Ohm's law, and doubling the voltage doubles the current for a given light intensity. By using several mercury batteries in series the voltage can be raised to a value that gives a suitably large needle deflection at the lowest levels of illumination likely to be encountered.

The darkroom safelights have to be switched off when using a photometer but it may be possible to screen the photocell in such a way that, while light from the enlarger lens can fall on it from above, light from the safelight cannot. In contriving this, care must be taken to avoid difficulties as regards seeing when the tone to be measured is located on the cell.

In view of the possible very high sensitivity of a particular cell, it should not be exposed to light while it is switched on until some experiments have been carried out to see what magnitude of needle deflection is likely to be obtained. If several hundreds of microamps flow through a small-range microammeter the needle will fly off the end of the scale, with possible damage to the delicate movement. Initially the cell should be kept covered, the current switched on, and the cell then gradually uncovered in ordinary tungsten room lighting is discover how sensitive the arrangement is.

It is necessary to find out the relationship between illumination on the cell and the scale-reading obtained, and this can be done with the aid of an enlarger fitted with a click-stop lens. With the meter shunt disconnected and the lens closed to its smallest aperture, a position on the column should be found for the enlarger that gives a small but readable needle deflection. The latter should be noted.

The lens is now opened up stop by stop and the meter reading recorded for each aperture. By the time a fairly large aperture is reached the needle is likely to reach the top end of the scale, and the shunt must now be connected across the meter. It should be noted that the relationship between the largest lens aperture and the next smaller one may not be a whole stop (e.g. f/4.5 and f/5.6), and this interval should be avoided, at least during the process of calibration.

As soon as the shunt is connected the needle deflection will drop, to give a reading of one-tenth its value with the shunt disconnected. The enlarger lens should now be stopped right down again and the enlarger head moved downwards to bring the meter needle to the same point on the scale as before stopping down. The lens can again be opened up stop by stop, noting the reading at each aperture as before, not forgetting to multiply by 10 to take the shunt into account.

The click stops on some enlarging lenses are not as accurate as they should be and if this is suspected to be the case with a particular lens the calibration of a photometer should be

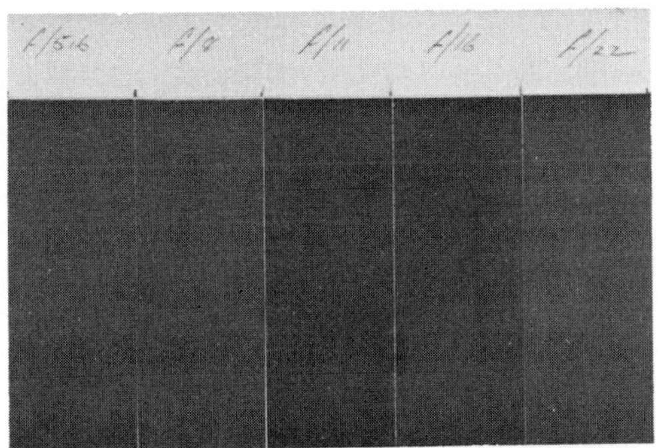

Fig. 5.6 The click stops on an enlarger lens may not be perfectly accurate. These tests show that f/11 and f/16 are in error, the apertures being too large. This is a very sensitive test especially if a hard grade of paper is used as was the case here.

checked by one of the other methods suggested in these pages.

We now have a series of relative illuminations as provided by the lens apertures, and the reading in microamperes corresponding to each stop. A graph can be plotted for log microamps against relative log illumination, and this should be a straight line. (Figure 5.7).

Such a graph has been plotted for two cells, and it is reproduced in these pages, One is a perfectly straight line and the other nearly so, but it will be noticed that the slopes of the two lines are different, one being much steeper than the other. The most convenient situation is where the current is directly proportional to the illumination, the graph for which is a straight line at 45°(assuming the same scale units for both axes) but whatever the slope, the. meter reading for any value of relative illumination can be determined from the graph.

A table can be compiled giving exposure times for any lens aperture for meter readings equivalent to one-third stop intervals and for one particular paper. There are, in fact, many ways in which meter readings can be converted to printing exposure times and the most satisfactory method will depend largely on the working methods of the individual.

In use, a selective photometer is positioned so that the photocell can be located to measure either the darkest or

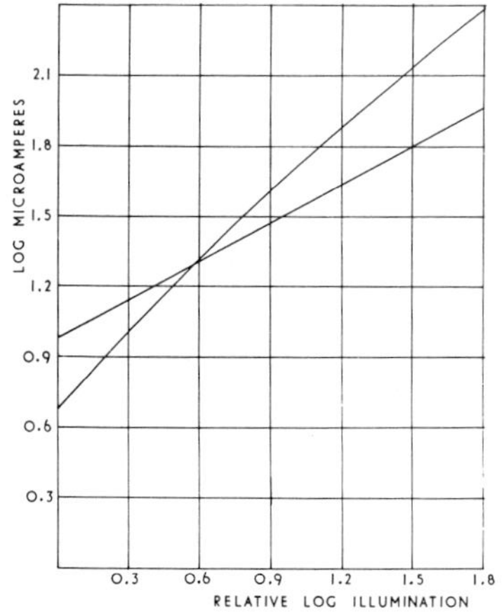

Fig. 5.7 Meter readings in log microamperes plotted against relative log illumination for two different CdS photocells.

lightest tone in the image. Once again, such a photometer can be employed as an integrating photometer simply by scrambling the light from the enlarger lens by means of a suitable diffusing material.

For the benefit of readers who prefer a cut and dried design to suggestions for experiment, here are some practical details of a selective photometer using a cadmium sulphide photoresistive cell and photographs of the actual instrument are reproduced in Figures 5.3 and 5.4. The 0 to 50 micro-ammeter is mounted on a sloping panel so that the scale can be read without difficulty in the darkroom and on the same panel is mounted the on-off switch and two sockets into which the photocell leads are plugged. Plugs to suit the sockets are attached to the twin wire from the cell.

There is, strictly, speaking, no necessity for an on-off switch as plugging in and unplugging the cell leads complete and break the circuit. It is convenient to include a switch however and it has the advantage that, by using a double-throw switch, the "off" position can be utilized for shorting the microammeter to damp the movement so that the photometer can be carried about without risk of damage to the moving coil mechanism.

The sloping panel forms the front of a plywood box that houses the few components and the battery. The latter is secured to the side of the box near the back by means of a Terry spring clip. Two strips of springy brass taken from an old dry battery serve to make contact with the positive metal case of the mercury battery and the top negative cap. One strip is secured to the bottom of the box and the other to one of the sides. The spring clip is located between the two contact strips.

In Figure 5.8 are two practical wiring diagrams. The first is a simple version embodying a series resistor to control the

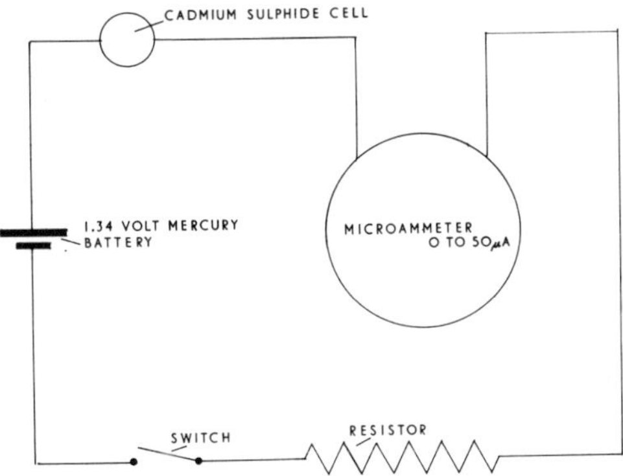

Fig. 5.8 Practical wiring diagram for a simple CdS enlarging exposure photometer.

maximum needle deflection. Its value is found by experiment. The second circuit embodies also a silicon diode that produces a more or less logarithmic scale as is explained on page 46.

For use on the enlarger baseboard the CdS cell can be mounted on the end of a narrow strip of wood or "Perspex" that serves as a probe. The method of mounting the cell depends on its type. A tubular cell in a glass envelope may be secured in a cartridge fuse-holder or some cells have pins that fit a miniature valve holder. A small flat cell may be cemented to a small panel of "Paxolin" using cellulose cement and wired to soldering tags attached to the panel. The panel is screwed to the probe.

About 2 ft of thin twin flex terminating in plugs to suit the sockets in the instrument panel is used to connect the cell to the microammeter circuit. The flex should be as soft and flexible as possible so that the cell will stay exactly where it is placed on the baseboard of the enlarger. Springy flex may pull a light-weight probe out of position.

A small cover fabricated of very thin plywood with an aperture in its top serves to screen the cell from all light except that from the enlarger lens as darkroom safelighting is powerful enough to affect the readings given by the photometer. In the absence of such screening it has been found that normal bromide safelight falling on the cell from a distance of 5 feet gives a reading of 5 microamperes using the circuitry as described. The design of the cover may have to be planned for individual safelight arrangements but, as a rule, these are such that little light falls on the enlarger easel.

It was mentioned earlier that the effective range of a 0 to 50 microammeter can be extended as required by the use of shunts across the meter coil. Such an expedient involves switching and there is always the risk of exposing the photocell to bright light when the shunt is disconnected with possible damage to the microammeter. A colleague who is expert in the field of electronics suggested that a more elegant method is to have a small silicon diode in the circuit. This has the effect of making the scale of the photometer approximately logarithmic so that a comparatively large range of brightnesses can be measured within the normal range of the microammeter.

The circuit in Figure 5.9 includes such a diode. The resistor in series with the meter and the diode can be adjusted within the limits of 10K to 20K ohms to control the magnitude of the needle deflection and in the case of the author's own instrument, a microammeter with a coil resistance of about 1,200 ohms called for a series resistor of 12K ohms to enable full-scale needle deflection to be obtained at the highest illumination ever likely to be encountered on the enlarger easel. There is no reason why a variable wire-wound 20K potentiometer should not be used, this being adjusted to suit individual requirements and then left undisturbed thereafter.

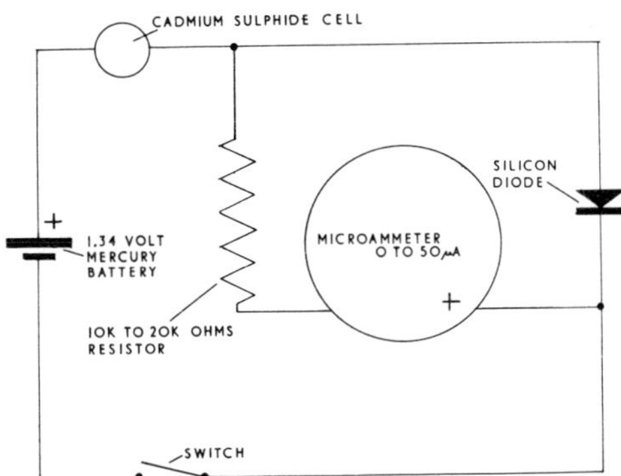

Fig. 5.9 This practical wiring diagram includes a silicon diode and a fixed resistor and the resulting instrument scale is approximately logarithmic.

In Figure 5.10 is a graph relating scale readings in micro-amps with relative log illumination on the CdS cell connected in series with a mercury cell and a microammeter but without a silicon diode. The parabolic curve means that if full-scale deflection is obtained for a high level of illumination on the enlarger easel, stopping down the lens aperture by aperture will reduce the meter reading as follows — 50, 25, 12½, 6¼ and so forth, or something very much like it. Thus, at the lower end of the meter scale, reducing the illumination by a given amount produces a very much smaller change in needle deflection than at the upper end. Reading accuracy at the lower end of the scale becomes poor.

The inclusion of a silicon diode in the circuit changes the shape of the response curve to that shown in Figure 5.11. The latter relates to a particular cell, meter and diode and, while the gradient of the curve changes throughout its length the relationship between illumination and scale reading is much more convenient than the one depicted by Figure 5.10. The scale becomes compressed at high levels of illumination but with readings approaching 50 micro-amperes it has been found that with papers of normal speeds,

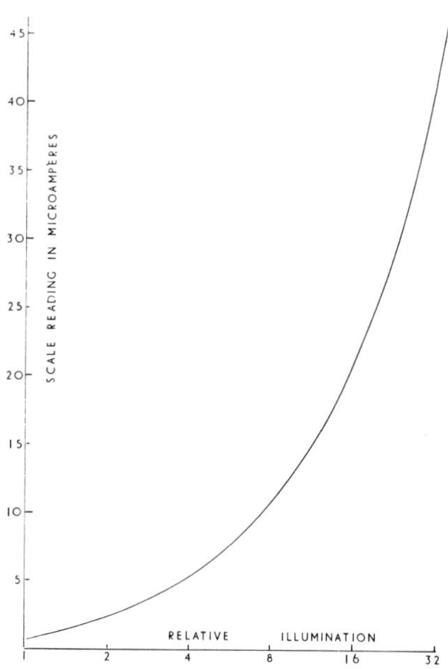

Fig. 5.10 Scale readings plotted against relative illumination for a CdS cell and microammeter with no silicon diode in the circuit.

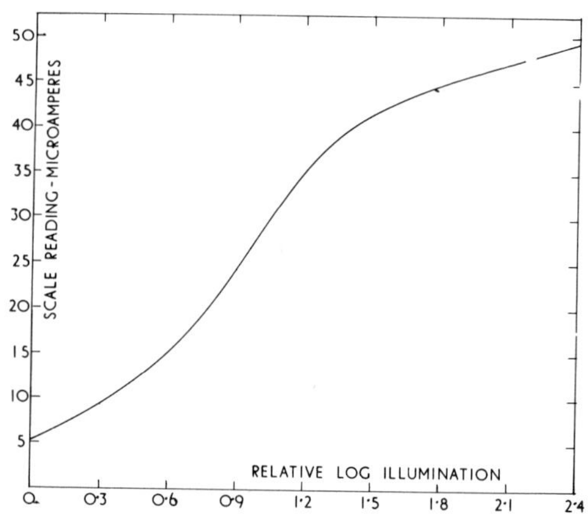

Fig. 5.11 A graph similar to that in Figure 5.10 but with a silicon diode in the circuit.

exposure times are uncontrollably short. The calibration of a photometer involves, in the first instance, the drawing of a graph like those in Figures 5.10 or 5.11, depending on whether or not a diode is included in the circuit. There is little difficulty in plotting such a curve as the intervals of 0.3 on the log illumination scale are equivalent to a series of lens apertures, f/4, f/5.6, f/8, f/11, f/16 and so on.

A wide range can be covered by altering the height of the enlarger half-way through the calibration procedure. It has been found that if several sets of meter readings are taken on different occasions but under the same conditions, they are very consistent which shows that the arrangement is adequately stable.

With the photometer described, the inclusion of a silicon diode in the circuit has resulted in full-scale needle deflection of 50 microamperes being obtained for an illumination of about 60 metre-candelas (6 foot-candelas). On the other hand, 1 metre-candela produces a reading of about 8 microamps and 0.25 metre-candelas a reading of 4 micro-amps. The high sensitivity at the low end of the scale is extremely useful because of the low levels of illumination often encountered in enlarging. At the same time, the compression towards the top of the scale reduces the chances of damage to the microammeter through the room lights being switched on inadvertently while the photometer is in active use.

A simple calculator for converting scale readings into exposure times is easily constructed to suit any particular photometer and any speed of paper. Its basis is a disc of card about 7 in. in diameter divided into 36 sectors each of 10°. Such a disc is shown in Figure 5.12 and it will be seen that the sectors are numbered in exposure times in seconds from $3\frac{1}{2}$ to 180 seconds. Such a range is likely to be big enough to satisfy all normal requirements. The series of numbers is in geometric progression with a common ratio of $\sqrt[6]{2}$ or 1.12 and the interval between one time and the next is thus equivalent to one-sixth of a stop. The numbers have been rounded off where necessary to give meaningful quantities. It will be noticed that a gap has been left between the ends of the scale. This is to draw attention to them so that there is little risk of misreading the calculator in this region.

A second card disc carries paper speed numbers from 3 to 20. These are arbitrary numbers and they are logarithmic in that an increase of three represents doubling of the speed. The range provided is large enough to cover available projection papers. The paper speed disc should be provided

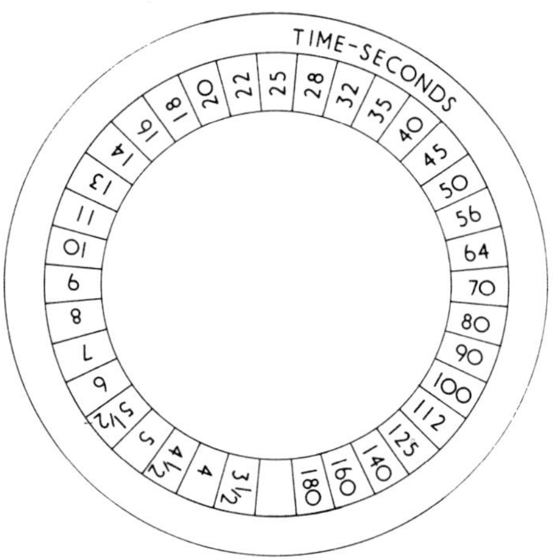

Fig. 5.12 The exposure time disc for a calculator for use with a CdS enlarging exposure photometer.

with a projecting tab about $\frac{1}{2}$ in. wide as this disc is only required to be moved when adjusting the general exposure levels as when setting up the photometer or after having replaced an enlarger lamp. The tab on the disc enables the latter to be fixed relative to the exposure time scale by means of an ordinary paper clip. (Figure 5.13).

The third disc is the same diameter as that carrying the paper speeds and its peripheral numbers are scale readings in microamps. These are read from the calibration graph at intervals of 0.05 along the relative log illumination axis. This conforms with the $\sqrt[6]{2}$ series of exposure times. (Figure 5.14).

The scale reading numbers will, of course, be peculiar to the reader's own photometer and the gap of one 10° sector has an aperture cut in it through which the paper speed numbers on the middle disc can be seen. The three discs are assembled concentrically by means of an eyelet through their centres. The assembly must be carried out with care so that the discs rotate easily but not too freely.

To set up the photometer for use, a good negative that will print well on a normal grade of paper and having important highlight and shadow detail should be enlarged, the exposure

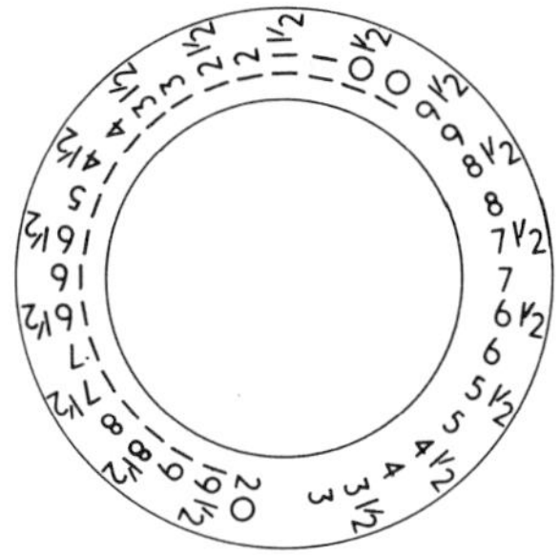

Fig. 5.13 *Paper speed disc for the enlarging exposure calculator.*

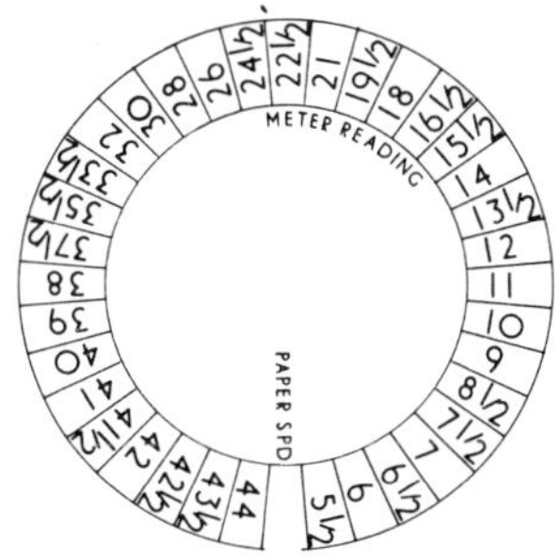

Fig. 5.14 *Calculator disc carrying the scale reading numbers.*

being determined by trial and error. Development should be carried out in fresh solution for a standard time of say 2 minutes at 68° F. Just before or after the print is exposed a suitable shadow or highlight area in the image should be measured with the photometer and the scale reading carefully noted. In the case of the Author's photometer a good print resulted from an exposure time of 5 seconds and the photometer reading for a shadow area was 32 microamps.

The upmost disc of the calculator is now rotated to bring the meter reading obtained opposite to the exposure time given to the trial print. It is now set for all prints on the particular paper used and the correct exposure time is shown opposite each scale reading. It is convenient to allot a speed number of 10 to the normal grade of paper in use and the paper speed disc can now be set to bring number 10 on the paper speed scale underneath the window in the top calculator disc.

At this point it is necessary to emphasise that the photometer described can be used for either shadow or highlight readings. In fact, it is feasible to change from one to the other to suit individual subjects but the speed number for any paper will depend on which of the two methods is used. A lower speed number is applicable to the shadow reading method than to the highlight method. There is a simple method of determining the shadow speed of a paper if its highlight speed is already known. Assume that a good print has been made on the basis of a highlight reading and that the calculator described previously was used to arrive at the exposure time. A shadow reading should now be taken with the photometer and the paper speed dial of the calculator rotated so that the shadow reading obtained gives the same exposure time as before. The speed number showing in the window is the shadow speed of the particular paper in use and it should be carefully recorded on the box or packet.

It may be found desirable to modify the calculator somewhat if it is intended to use it for highlight and shadow reading methods as seems to be appropriate. Instead of calibrating all three scales to one-sixth stop intervals they should be numbered at one-third stop intervals. These modified scales are shown in Figure 5.15. The paper speed scale is now numbered from 1 to 30 and this is sufficient to accommodate both highlight and shadow speeds of all the papers in use. As the relationship between highlight and shadow speed of a paper depends on its exposure range, the softer the grade the bigger the interval between the two speed numbers, it may be found desirable to set the arbitrary highlight speed of the normal paper at a figure higher than the 10 suggested earlier — 20 may be found

better. If this is not done it may be found that the shadow
speed of a paper is less than 1 — a negative number in fact.

By placing a diffuser over the enlarger lens while taking
readings the photometer can be used as an integrating instrument and the integrating method calls for yet another level
of speed number for every paper. This will be between the

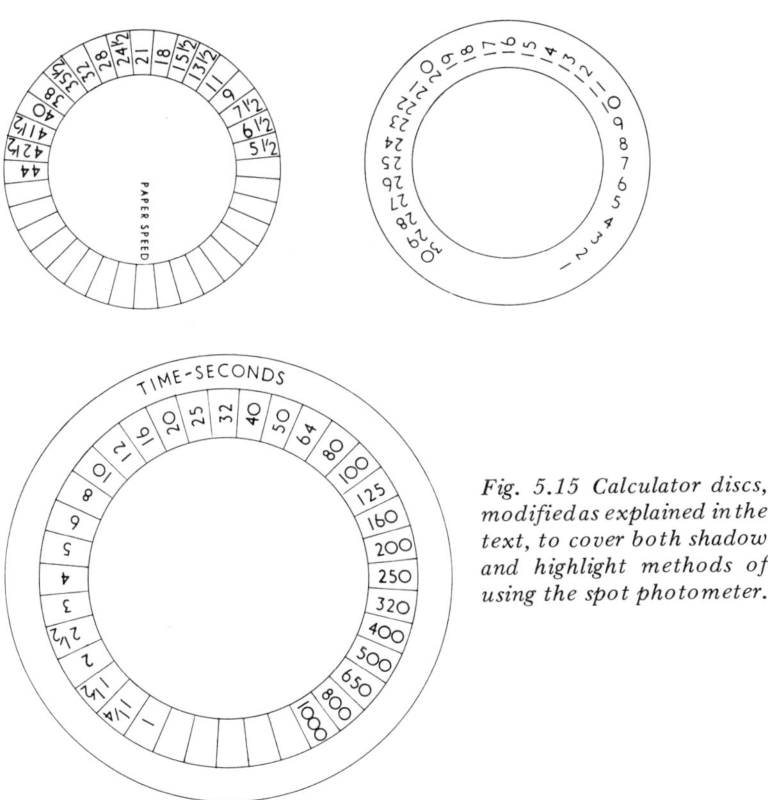

Fig. 5.15 Calculator discs,
modified as explained in the
text, to cover both shadow
and highlight methods of
using the spot photometer.

highlight and shadow speed numbers. In a later chapter a
simple method is described with which paper speeds on any
basis may be determined quickly and accurately.

For the benefit of readers who enjoy experiment it is
proposed to describe a sensitive long-range photometer based
on a CdS cell. This can be used for spot readings of shadows

or highlights on the enlarger baseboard and for this purpose the cell should be a small one of less than $\frac{1}{2}$ in. in diameter and masked down to a size small enough for reliable spot measurements. The same construction as suggested for the earlier photometer described is suitable. In Chapter 8 suggestions are made for using the same circuitry for integrated measurements, the photocell being built into a home-made paper holder and masking board.

There are several important qualities to look for in a system for the photometric determination of enlarging exposures, these quite apart from accuracy, which is an obvious requirement. High sensitivity is desirable to deal with the occasional big enlargement from a dense negative exposed at a small aperture as say when the masking board has been tilted to correct converging verticals in an architectural shot. A wide range is also needed; in fact, much larger than is usually found in commercial instruments of modest price.

The CdS cell offers high sensitivity without the need for amplification of the current flowing through the cell but even this may be found deficient under really adverse enlarging conditions. Two trial enlargements, have just been made, one from a really dense negative at 15 diameters with the lens stopped down to f/22. On Kodak normal bromide paper the exposure time was 240 seconds. At the other end of the scale a thin negative was enlarged three diameters and the exposure made at f/5.6 on the same grade of paper. An exposure time of only $\frac{1}{2}$ second was required. These two examples, which are extreme, indicate that a photometer with a range of at least 500 to 1 is desirable, equivalent to nine lens stops — not far short of three decades.

There is no problem in measuring the light on the easel where exposures are of moderate length but adequate sensitivity coupled with satisfactory accuracy is not easy to achieve at low levels. Extreme sensitivity with a CdS cell seems to be accompanied always by sluggish response at low levels and this feature is better avoided if possible.

A circuit for a CdS enlarging photometer is shown in Figure 5.16. It goes further than the simplest basic circuit as it incorporates three variable resistors, one in series with the cell and microammeter and the other two as shunts across the microammeter. The series resistor of about 100K ohms maximum enables the needle deflection to be restricted at high light levels without materially affecting the deflections at low levels. The current flow recorded by the microammeter depends on the total resistance of the circuit and at low light levels where the CdS cell resistance may be hundreds

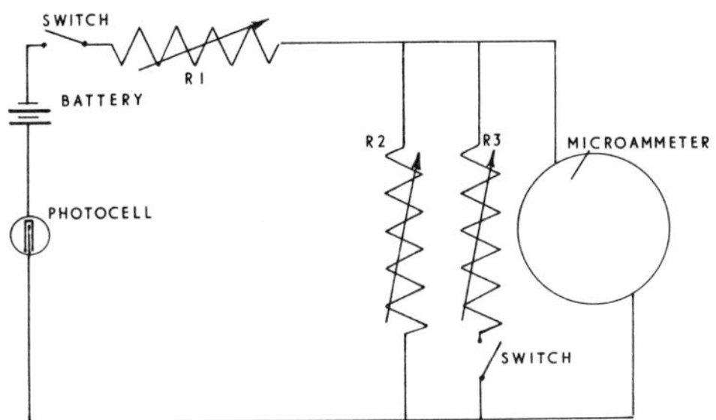

Fig. 5.16 Circuit for CdS photometer embodying variable resistors for use in a long range photometer.

of thousands of ohms the addition of the series resistor is insignificant. At high levels of illumination the circuit resistance falls to about that of the series resistor and the coil of the meter and the value of these will control the maximum current that can flow even if the light is so bright that the cell resistance approaches zero. Too high a value of series resistor will make the top end of the scale so crowded that reading accuracy is poor.

A variable shunt with a maximum value of between $\frac{1}{2}$ and 1 megohm enables small adjustments to be made of the calibration level should the need arise. For example, an enlarger lamp may emit yellower light as it ages or it may be necessary to adjust for batch-to-batch variations in the speeds of papers.

The second shunt having a maximum value equal to about one-fifth the resistance of the microammeter is to give a suitable range shift round about X10 as it is hardly feasible to fit a 9-stop range within the length of the meter scale. This shunt is adjusted to give the required range shift and is then left untouched. It is controlled by an on-off switch which provides the change of range.

The circuit described calls for a series resistor to restrict the deflection at high light levels and a high-value shunt in the form of a variable resistor for carrying out small calibration level adjustments. The settings of these two involve some trial and error so that the following requirements are met. We require full-scale needle deflection under the conditions necessitating minimum exposure times and a setting of the shunt (R2 in Figure 5.16) such that turning the resistance to its full value gives a needle movement off the end of the scale equivalent to about a stop. The needle of most microammeters are free to move a small distance off the top end of the scale. Decreasing the value of this shunt will, of course, bring the needle deflection towards zero. A rough preliminary calibration may be necessary to establish the needle shift at the top end of the scale which is equivalent of about one stop.

It is now possible to establish the meter readings for a series of light intensities varying by a factor of 2. If full-scale needle deflection is obtained at f/5.6 the click stops on the lens can be employed to determine the readings at f/8, f/11, f/16, and f/22 — a range of four stops. A further stop can be obtained by the use of a neutral density filter having a value of 0.3. This is placed over the cell so that it is completely covered and it reduces the light to exactly one-half.

To make the foregoing procedure clear, as it may sound somewhat complicated the following readings were obtained for the initial calibration with the shunt in circuit:—

f/5.6	48 microamperes
f/8	35 ,,
f/11	25 ,,
f/16	17 ,,
f/22	13 ,,
f/22 with 0.3 N.D.	6 ,,
f/22 with 0.6 N.D.	3 ,,

Intermediate readings can be obtained so that exposures can be determined to within one-third of a stop if one has a neutral density filter of 0.1 available. For example, at f/5.6 the reading was 48 on the scale; a neutral density of 0.1 over the cell will reduce the needle deflection to a value equivalent to one-third of a stop smaller than f/5.6. With the lens set at f/8 and with the 0.1 N.D. filter over the cell, the lens aperture is adjusted to bring the needle to 35 microamps. If the N.D. filter is now removed, the new reading is equivalent to one-third of a stop larger than f/8. A less precise but quite adequate method is to interpolate visually after the single stop intervals have been established.

Calibration has also to be carried out with the range shift shunt out of circuit. If this gives a X10 shift as regards current it must not be assumed that it is also a X10 shift in light values. For this reason the calibration with no shunt has to be dealt with in exactly the same way as with the shunt but at a lower general level of illumination as provided by a denser negative at a bigger degree of enlargement. In Figure 5.17 the two broken curves show the

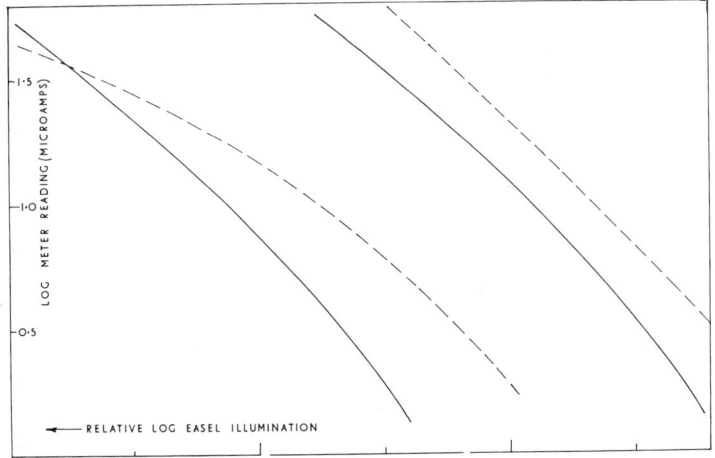

Fig. 5.17 Approximate calibration curves for the author's CdS photometer using a light-collecting lens system let into the enlarger masking board. The two broken curves are for a X10 shunt across the microammeter and the solid curves are for a range-shift method utilising a 1.0 neutral density filter.

relationship between light on the easel and meter reading with and without a X10 shunt and it will be seen that with no shunt the relationship between log meter is a linear one.

At this stage some photographic tests will show the relationship between meter readings and exposure times. It is a simple matter to provide the microammeter with an additional scale on clear film attached to the glass and this can be made to read directly in exposure times. Using a shunt for range shifting will almost certainly involve making a double scale. This may prove difficult to read unless it is carefully drawn as the illumination of the meter causes shadows to be cast on the meter scale proper and the result can be confusing.

CHAPTER SIX

INTEGRATING ENLARGING PHOTOMETRY

Before discussing integrating enlarging photometers as such it is important to examine what they measure, how they base their indicated exposures and how reliable they are. There is a widespread belief that they are extremely unreliable but this opinion is generally founded on little more than instinct. It can be shown that such a meter can give very good results indeed.

Looking again at Figure 1.1 on page 2 it will be seen that the D_{min} and D_{max} of the negative are located at the upper and lower limiting points on the paper curve by a suitable printing exposure. Additionally, the density range of the negative should match the log exposure range of the paper. This is a greatly simplified picture of the sensitometry of printing but it suffices for the explanation that follows.

Somewhere between the D_{min} and D_{max} of a negative lies a density value equal to the integrated or total density $(\overline{D})$. There may be no tone in the negative having a density equal to $\overline{D}$ but this has no significance. It will be appreciated that the distance on the log exposure axis of the paper curve between the $\overline{D}$ and D_{min} of the negative has an important bearing on the validity of printing exposures estimated from $\overline{D}$. If $\overline{D} - D_{min}$ is predictable for all negatives the printing exposures based on $\overline{D}$ will be as valid as those based on D_{min} or D_{max}. (Figure 6.1).

In the first instance let us consider what might be called a "linear" negative — one in which all tones have equal areas and having a large number of different tones between D_{min}

     Exposure Control in Enlarging

and D_{max}. The obvious example of such a negative is a stepped or continuous wedge, the former being a commonly-used device in photography. The value of $\overline{D} - D_{min}$ for such a linear negative can be calculated and its value depends only on the difference between the minimum and maximum densities of the wedge or negative—$D_{max} - D_{min}$. In Figure

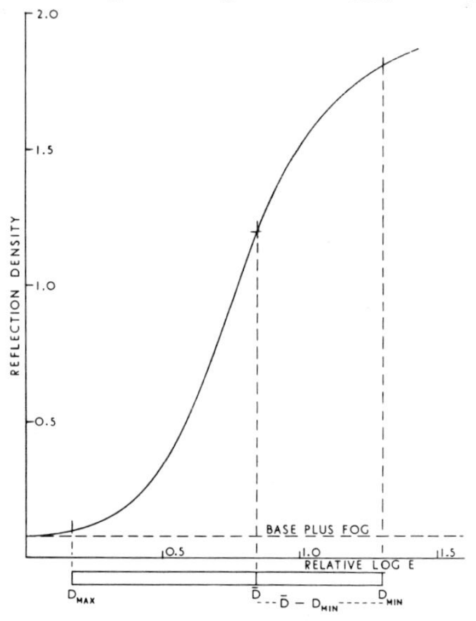

Fig. 6.1 The value of $\overline{D} - D_{min}$ ($\Delta\overline{D}$) *has an important bearing on the validity of total density as a criterion for printing exposure estimation.*

6.2 $\overline{D} - D_{min}$ has been plotted against density range for values of the latter between zero and 2.5. The quantity, $\overline{D} - D_{min}$ has been abbreviated to $\Delta\overline{D}$ for the sake of brevity.

It will be seen from Figure 6.2 that $\Delta\overline{D}$ increases with increasing density range of the negative. Hence, the interval between $\overline{D}$ and D_{min} varies with negative contrast, being lower for a soft negative than for a hard one. At the same time, the log exposure range of the printing paper increases with negative contrast, a soft negative calling for a paper with a short exposure range and a hard negative requiring a paper with a long exposure range. To see if there is any consistency regarding the location of the $\overline{D}$ of a negative on the characteristic curve of a paper in correctly exposed prints, a series of imaginary papers having perfectly straight curves was considered. Two paper surfaces were considered also, a smooth glossy and a smooth matt as the maximum density of a paper depends very much on its surface. These hypothetical characteristic curves are shown in Figure 6.3 and it will be seen that the log exposure ranges of both the matt and glossy

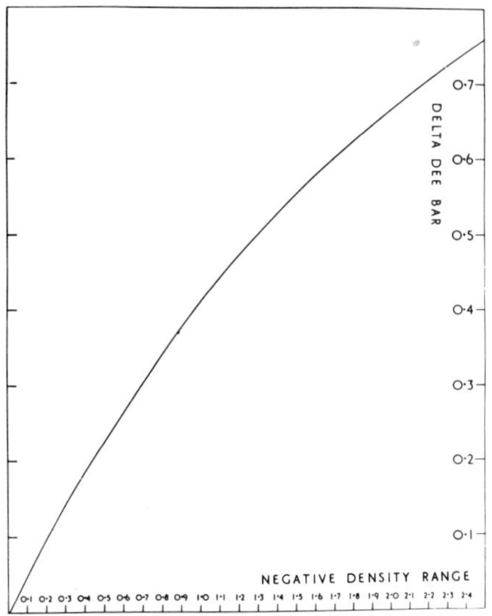

Fig. 6.2 $\overline{D} - D_{min}$ *plotted against nagative density range. Its value increases with increasing density range.*

papers depicted range from very small to very large. For the sake of argument it was assumed that a good print utilises the whole of the paper curve which would be the case if actual curves were straight throughout their lengths.

From the maximum density of each paper a distance equal to $\Delta\overline{D}$ was measured to the left for negatives fitting each paper log exposure range. Perpendiculars were then dropped as shown to locate the $\overline{D}$ of each negative on all the paper curves. The location varied from between 1.0 and 1.2 above base and fog for the glossy papers which covered log exposure ranges from 0.6 to 1.6 (4—1 to 40—1). For smooth matt papers the location of negative $\overline{D}$ is at a density of between 0.65 and 0.75 above base and fog.

It is obviously not sufficient to rely on formalised characteristic curves like those in Figure 6.3, and curves of actual papers were then substituted for them. Some of the curves used for the purpose were plotted by the author and others were provided by the research laboratories of Ilford Ltd. and Kodak Ltd. It was found that the placing of the $\overline{D}$ of

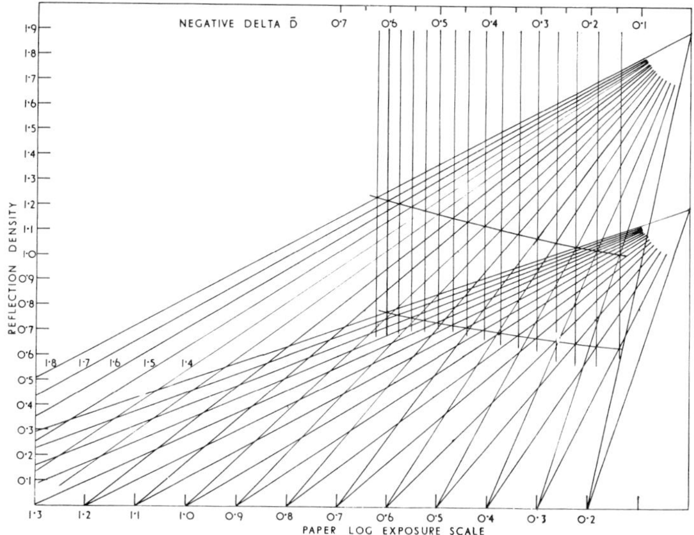

Fig. 6.3 Formalised paper curves for glossy and smooth matt papers showing the location of the $\overline{D}$ of linear negatives on the appropriate grade of paper.

negatives in correctly exposed prints was in close agreement with that using formalised curves. It may be concluded that in correctly exposed prints, the $\overline{D}$ of the negatives are located at a density of about 1.1 above base in the case of glossy papers and about 0.70 above base and fog with smooth matt papers. When using semi-glossy papers such as velvet, the location of the $\overline{D}$ of negatives may be assumed to be at a density between 0.70 and 1.10.

It may be argued that when using an integrating enlarging exposure meter, paper speed numbers should be based on the xposure required to produce a density of 1.10 for glossy papers and 0.70 for smooth matt. Extensive experimental work has shown this to be true but no substantial errors result from using speed numbers based on any arbitrary middle density. Speed numbers based on a very low or very high density are unsuitable for use with an integrating meter.

It is fairly obvious that negatives of actual scenes as distinct from step-wedges are often far from linear in that the areas of the various tones may be far from equal. (Figure 6.4). To

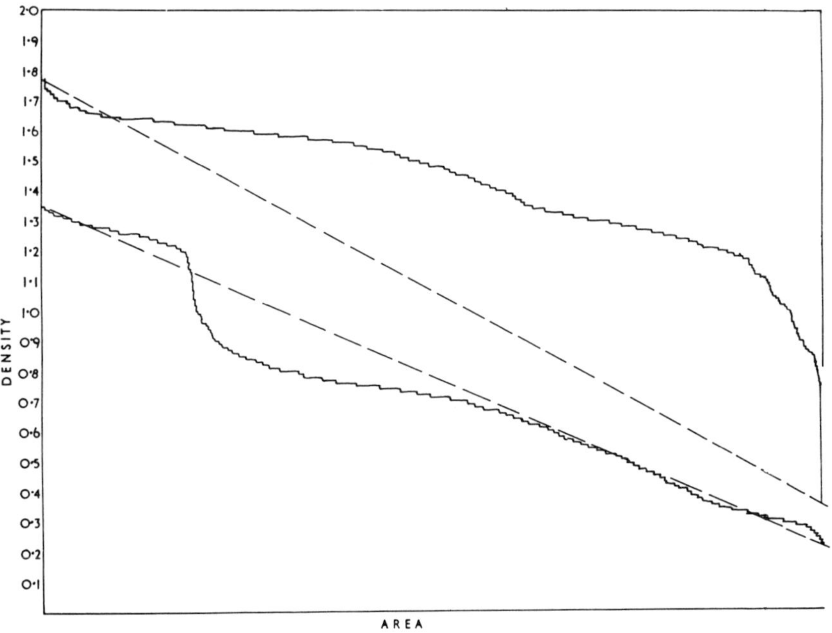

Fig. 6.4 Plots of two negatives, one that is nearly linear and the other far from linear.

examine this, several hundreds of negatives, selected at random and embracing all kinds of subjects both indoor and out, were measured to discover their minimum and maximum densities and also their total or integrated densities. From these data their density ranges $(D_{max} - D_{min})$ were calculated and also their values of $\Delta\bar{D}$ $(\bar{D} - D_{min})$.

In Figure 6.5 the actual values of $\Delta\bar{D}$ for 200 varied negatives are shown plotted against negative density range. The curve represents the theoretical values of $\Delta\bar{D}$ and is identical with the curve in Figure 6.1. As might be expected, actual negatives depart radically from the theoretical values of $\Delta\bar{D}$ but it should be noted that, in Figure 6.5, the vertical scale has been extended by a factor of 4 relative to the horizontal scale in order to accommodate the large number of plot points. This scale expansion magnifies the differences between the theoretical and actual values of $\Delta\bar{D}$.

From Figure 6.5 it is apparent that printing exposures based on the $\bar{D}$ of negatives will be incorrect nearly as often as they are correct. Only negatives of which the $\Delta\bar{D}$ plot falls on the curve will be correctly exposed and the further the plot point of a negative from the curve the larger the error in the indicated exposure. If the actual value of $\Delta\bar{D}$ differs from the theoretical value by 0.3, this means an exposure error of one lens stop. If the actual value is larger than the theoretical value the error will produce over-exposure of the print; if it is smaller, the resulting print will be under-exposed. To illustrate this graphically, two further curves have been added to Figure 6.5 to produce Figure 6.6. The added curves are 0.3 log units above and below the original curve.

It will be seen that only one or two isolated negatives fall outside the area bounded by the two additional curves and these particular negatives were quite extreme as regards density distribution. Those at the bottom of the diagram had very large and empty shadow areas while those at the top had very big areas of dense highlights.

An error of plus or minus a stop in printing exposures is much too large for any measurement system giving rise to it to have much practical value. There is, however, an important factor to be taken into account. This is the "development amplitude" of printing papers. In Figure 6.7 is shown a family of characteristic curves of a typical modern bromide paper for different times of development. During the early stages of development the slope of the curve increases rapidly. After a certain development time which is usually about $1\frac{1}{4}$ minutes, the curve reaches

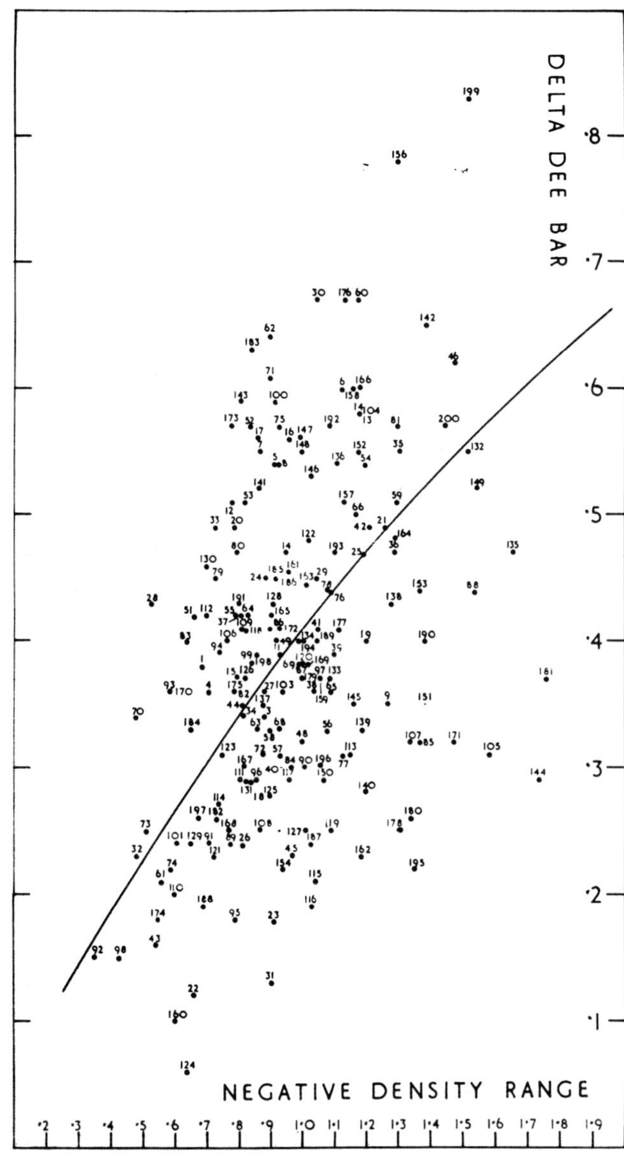

Fig. 6.5 Actual values of $\Delta\overline{D}$ for 200 negatives plotted against negative density range. The curve shows the theoretical values of $\Delta\overline{D}$ for linear negatives.

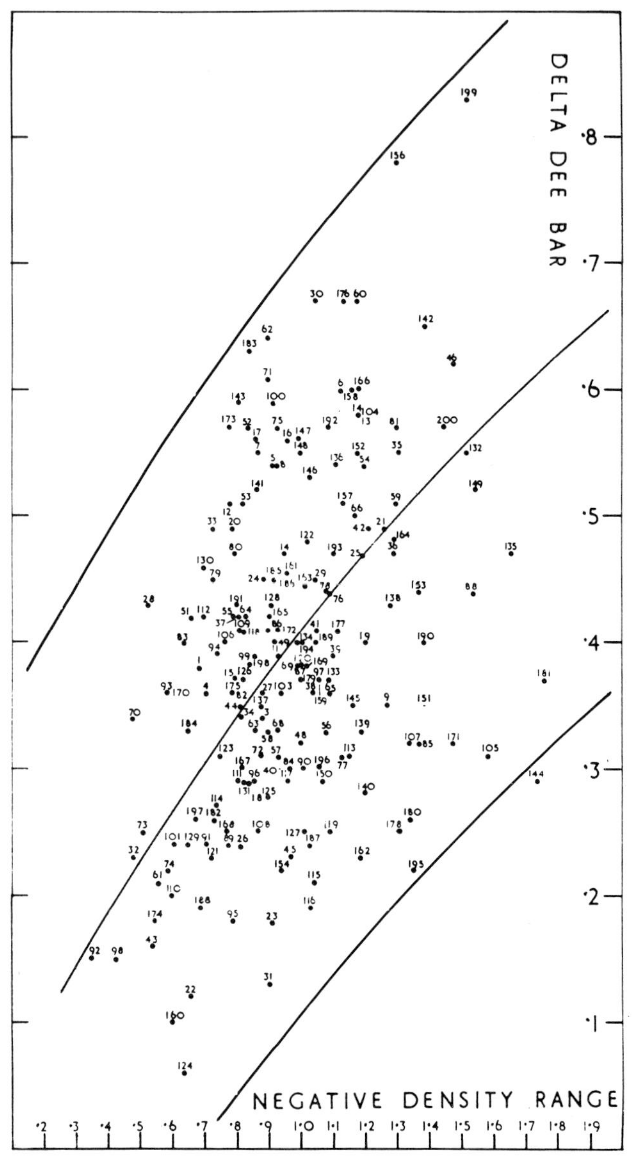

Fig. 6.6 The two additional curves have been drawn at 0.3 log units above and below the middle curve. Any prints from negatives with plots outside the added curves will be over- or under-exposed by up to one stop if their printing exposures are based on total density.

equilibrium shape and further development produces no increase in slope and no increase in maximum density. The curve does however move slowly to the left with increasing development and this indicates a progressive increase in effective speed. The effective speed of a paper is, in fact, lower for short development times than for long ones. Eventually, of course, with greatly prolonged development, there is the onset of objectionable fogging or staining. Within the practical limits of development, usually $1\frac{1}{2}$ to 4 minutes, any time is as good as any other, provided that the

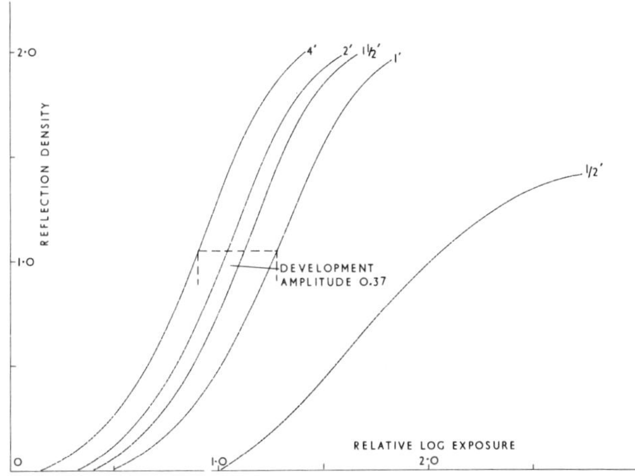

Fig. 6.7 A set of characteristic curves for different degrees of development for a typical bromide paper. The distance between the extreme curves with equilibrium shape, measured on the log exposure axis, is the development amplitude of the paper.

printing exposure is a suitable one for the development time given.

Taking the curves of equilibrium shape, the horizontal distance in log exposure units, between the two outermost curves is a measure of the development amplitude of the paper. The magnitude of development amplitude depends on the make and type of paper, and is affected also by the contrast grade although not in a wholly predictable manner. On average, development amplitude varies from 0.25 to 0.35 of which the average is 0.3. This value means that printing exposures can vary over a range of 2 to 1 and with an appropriate time of development, a good print will result. The idea that a printing paper should be developed to "finality" is completely wrong especially with modern papers which contain at least a small proportion of silver chloride. The rapid chlorobromide papers such as Kodak "Bromesko" and the discontinued Ilford "Plastika" have rather bigger development amplitudes than the pure bromide papers but the true bromide paper is now rare or even extinct.

In Figure 6.8 two further curves have been added to Figure 6.5. These are 0.15 log units vertically above and below the middle curve and these curves represent the limits of the development possible with the average modern paper. All the negatives of which the plots fall within the area bounded by these curves will yield good prints if they are exposed on the basis of $\overline{D}$ provided that the development is adjusted to produce images of satisfactory density. This simple expedient covers the majority of actual negatives. It was stated earlier that the 200 negatives measured were selected at random but this is not quite true. In going through several thousands of negatives, any with noticeably uneven density distribution were extracted and, as a result, the sampling embraced an unnaturally large proportion of non-typical subjects.

Negatives falling within the shaded area in Figure 6.8 can be printed satisfactorily on the basis of $\overline{D}$ provided a suitable correction factor is applied to the exposure time indicated by the integrating photometer. Half a stop more exposure for negatives with very large areas of shadow and half a stop more for negatives with very large highlight areas are adequate correction except for the most extreme negatives. The author has found it necessary to search diligently for negatives that fall outside the area bounded by the two outer curves in Figure 6.8. If correction such as has been suggested is applied to borderline cases it does not matter, the development amplitude of the paper will take care of any error.

The measurement of the $\Delta\overline{D}$ of many hundreds of negatives and making prints from them has justified the author's confidence in printing estimation based on integrated measurements of the brightness of the image on the enlarger easel

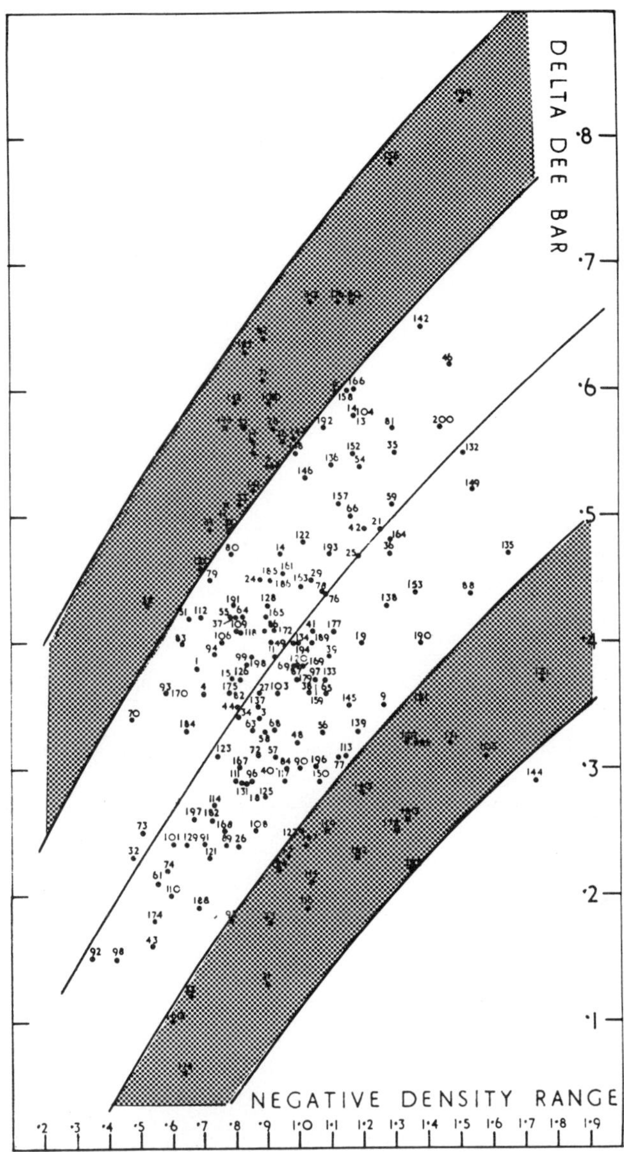

Fig. 6.8 The two curves 0.15 log units above and below the middle one represent the average limits of the development amplitude of the printing paper. All negatives within the area bounded by them will be correctly exposed on the basis of negative total density provided prints are developed by inspection for a time that gives satisfactory density.

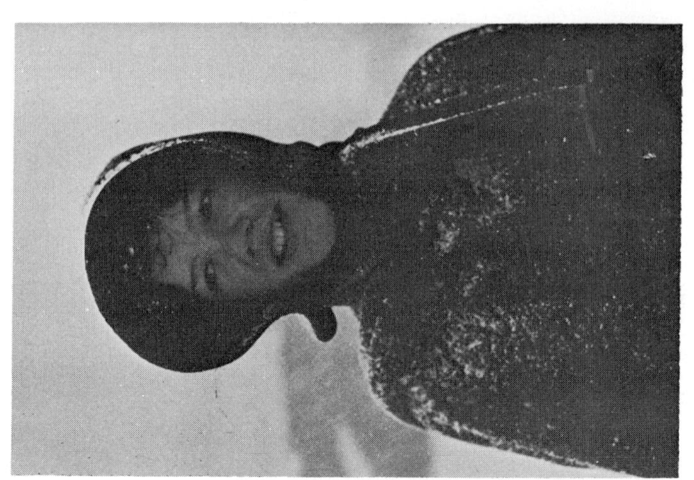

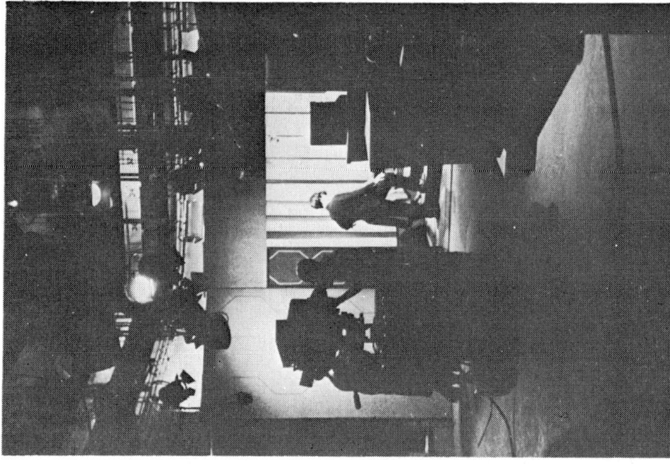

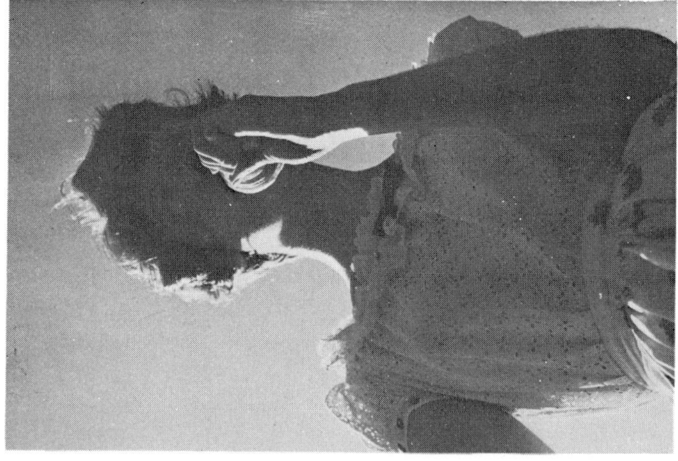

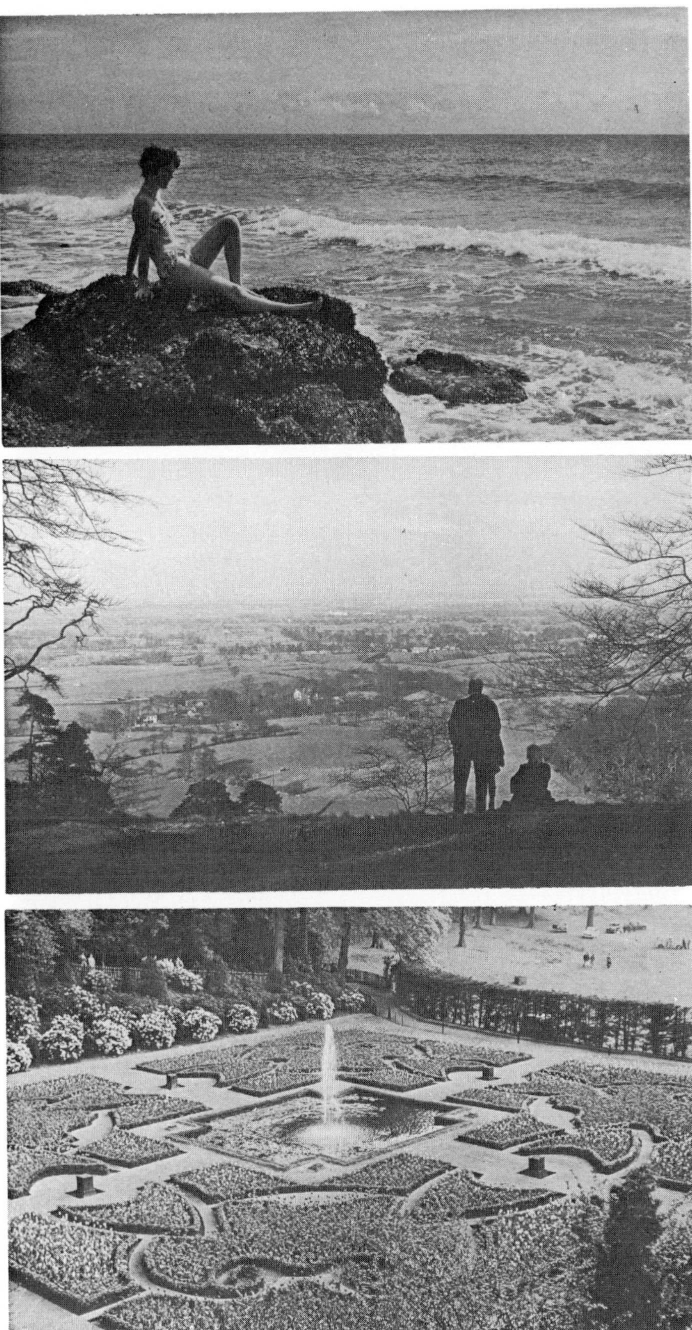

Fig. 6.9 These prints were made using an integrating photometer for estimating exposures. Despite the different density distributions of the negatives all the indicated exposures were correct within the development amplitudes of the four grades of paper used.

which is equivalent to measuring the total density of the negative. The fact that indicated exposures have to be corrected in the case of negatives with very unbalanced density distributions is of little consequence in practice as the need for correction can be seen at a glance when inspecting the image on the enlarger baseboard.

CHAPTER SEVEN

COMMERCIAL INTEGRATING ENLARGING PHOTOMETERS

The least expensive integrating enlarging exposure meter is the Paterson Enlarging Computer and it is illustrated on page 74. It is essentially a cadmium sulphide photocell in front of which is a rotatable disc with an annular tapered slot that passes in front of the cell. The device is mains operated and in use it is placed on the enlarger baseboard immediately below the lens. A diffusing screen of matt plastic in a circular holder is placed in front of the lens to scramble the light and the disc on the photometer is rotated slowly to vary the amount of light falling on the cell. A point is found at which a neon glowlamp just strikes and the printing exposure time required is read off from the scale on the instrument dial. The scale is adjustable to enable papers of different speeds to be used.

As with all on-easel photometry the safelights must be switched off while readings are being taken as even a small amount of extraneous light on the cell will invalidate the readings. The effective range of the Paterson meter for a fixed paper speed is about 8 to 1. This is not large enough for many purposes and under extreme conditions, as when enlarging a dense negative to a big size, it may be necessary to determine the exposure required with the lens wide open even if it is proposed to stop the lens down for making the exposure.

The simplicity and low cost of the Paterson Enlarging Computer will commend itself to those who want a reliable

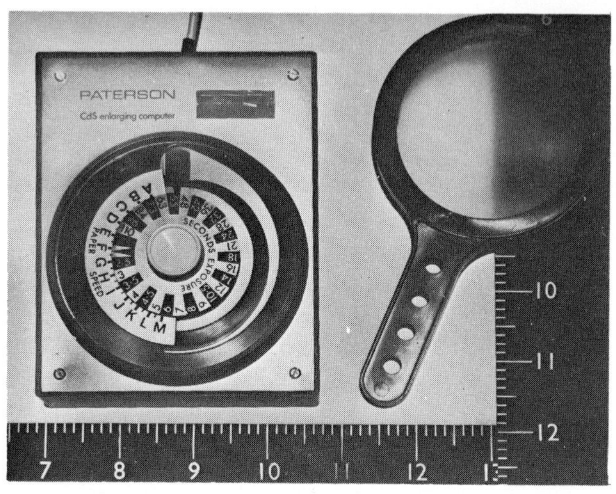

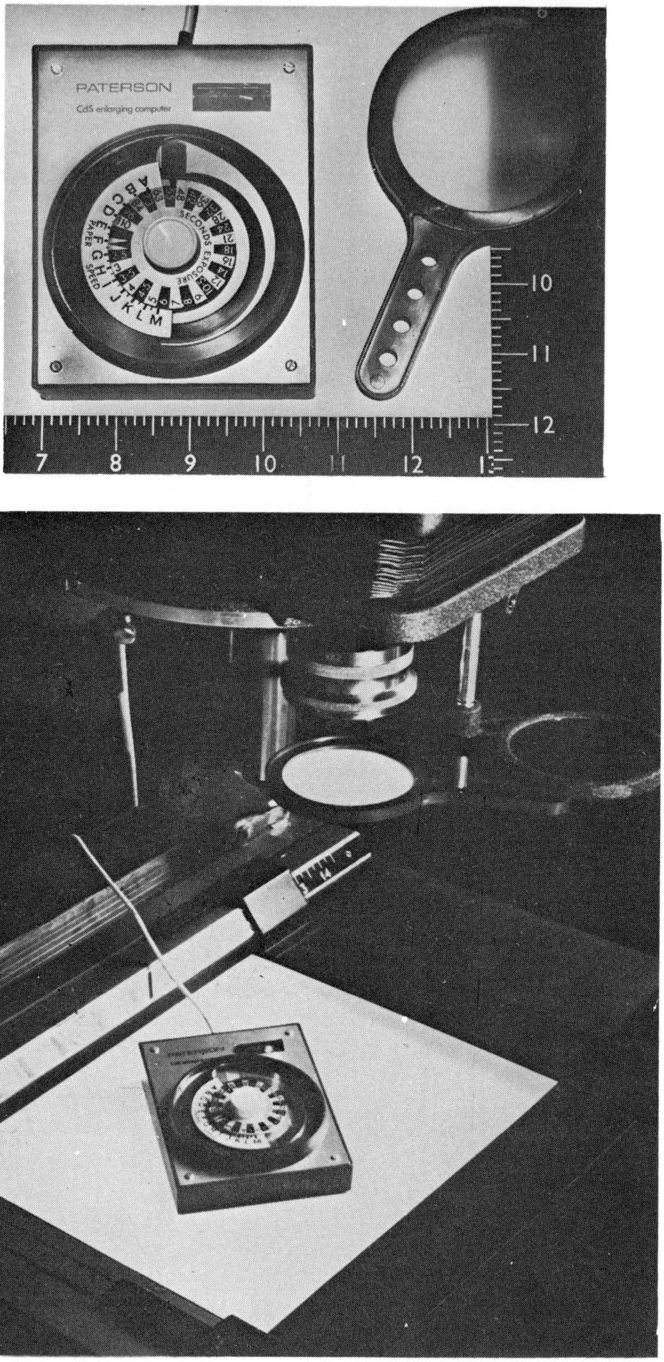

Fig. 7.1 The Paterson enlarging computer showing the matt plastic light scrambler and also the instrument in use on an enlarger.

means of determining enlarging exposure times under routine printing conditions. It has been found to be very reliable.

A somewhat unusual integrating enlarging photometer is the "Revomatic" exposure evaluator for enlargers to give it its full title. It is made by John Blishen & Co., Ltd. of 75 Kilburn Lane, London, W. 10 and it takes the form of a masking board paper holder accommodating paper up to 8 x 10 in. A larger version taking up to 10 x 12 in. has been developed. Within the masking board is housed the electronics responsible for measuring the exposing light and controlling the exposure time.

A specially selected and treated Telefunken photocell in a small enclosure supported above the surface of the printing paper but out of the light beam from the enlarger lens collects the light reflected by the printing paper while it is being exposed and when enough light has fallen on the paper the enlarger lamp is switched off automatically.

An adjustment for various paper speeds is provided and this has two overlapping ranges controlled by a switch. The speed setting is accurately calibrated in 15-per cent increments.

In use, the operator focuses his negative in the usual way and selects the lens aperture it is proposed to use for the exposure. The appropriate paper speed is selected and a sheet of paper placed in position under the mask. A touch on a button starts the exposure and at the same time switches off the enlarger safelights, the latter being powered from a socket at the rear of the masking board. At the end of the exposure the enlarger lamp is switched off and the safelights automatically switched on.

It has been found that the photocell used in this equipment is highly sensitive to blue light but it has low sensitivity to red. This means that, provided the darkroom safelights are not close to the enlarger easel, there may be no need to arrange to have them switched off during exposures. A simple test is described in the instructions to determine whether or not the safelight illumination is affecting the duration of exposure.

An interesting aspect of the "Revomatic" is the effect of shading and printing-up on the duration of exposures. If, for example, a dark shadow is held back during part of the exposure the rest of the image will be given more exposure than it would receive if no shading were undertaken. This may be all to the good if the negative being printed has particularly empty shadows and dense highlights but some experience is needed to use this feature to advantage. Like all methods of exposure estimation by measurement the exposures indicated are those appropriate for straight prints. Any local exposure control has to be exercised by the printer.

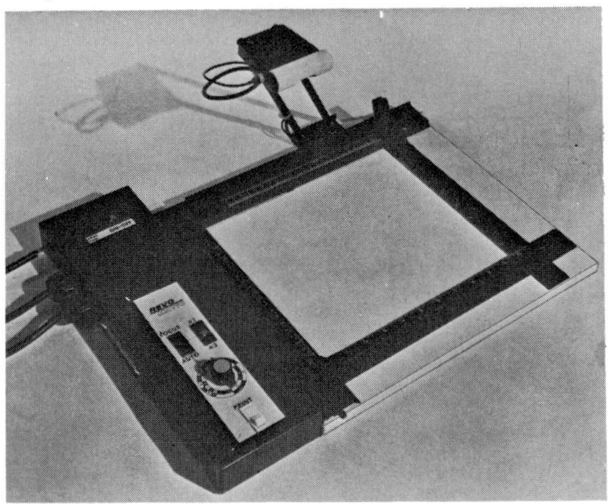

Fig. 7.2 The "Revomatic" masking board enlarging exposure meter (model 2).

When using the "Revomatic", paper speeds are best determined by making trial prints on the several grades of paper in use. Wedge tests may not be very informative because the reflectivity of the paper surface has an effect on the lengths of the exposures given. A paper with an ivory base for example will have a higher effective speed than one with a perfectly white base although the emulsions may be identical. At the same speed setting the ivory paper will be given a longer exposure than the white one and hence, to correct this, a higher speed setting must be used for the tinted paper.

The Agfa "Variomat" works on similar principles but the light passing through the printing paper during exposure is measured and this controls the duration of the exposure. Both the "Revomatic" and the "Variomat" are claimed to be suitable for exposure determination in colour printing by the white-light method.

CHAPTER EIGHT

HOME-MADE INTEGRATING ENLARGING METERS

An ordinary photo-electric exposure meter such as the Weston Master can be used as the basis of a simple densitometer for measuring the total densities of negatives. All that is required is a bench, sloping or vertical, for holding the meter, the negative in a masked carrier or on a masked stage, and a suitable lamp on a movable carriage. (Figure 8.1).

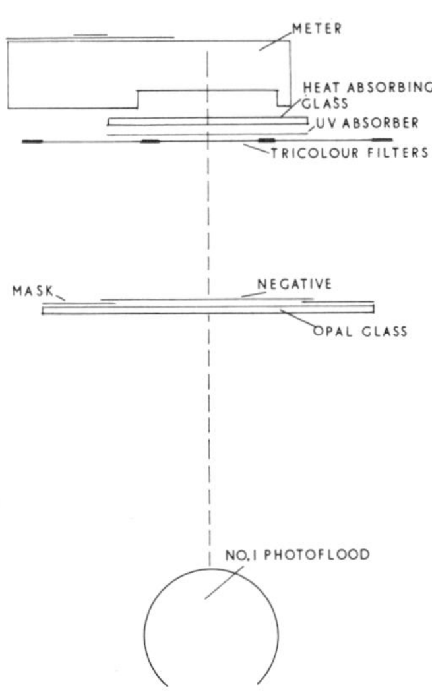

Fig. 8.1 Schematic arrangement of light source and Weston Master exposure meter for use as an integrating enlarging exposure meter.

The author has constructed several of such optical benches and the latest version is illustrated on page 79. This is arranged vertically as this has been found more convenient than a sloping bench in that the stage for negatives is horizontal and films do not have to be held in a carrier. A film is just laid on the stage, making sure that the mask on the stage cuts out all the clear rebates, and it will stay put for long enough for its density to be measured. If a film has a marked tendency to curl it may be necessary to hold it flat with a sheet of clear glass laid on top of it.

The negative stage must be provided with a sheet of flashed opal glass so that the density measured is diffuse total density. If clear glass is used for the stage the measurement is rather of specular total density and the readings obtained may be misleading where exposures are being determined for a diffused light or condenser and opal lamp enlarger. If the light scattered by the negative is not collected and evaluated, density readings will tend to be high and this inflation is more pronounced with negatives containing large dense areas such as skies. It is such negatives that tend to indicate excessively large printing exposures on the basis of total density and they will be larger still if specular rather than diffuse density is measured.

Although the densitometer illustrated is intended for measurement of black and white negatives it has all the necessary facilities for the measurement of the blue, green and red light transmissions of colour negatives. There is a slide to take a card mount carrying suitable tricolour filters and there is a space below the exposure meter sufficient to take a UV-absorbing gelatine filter and a heat-absorbing filter.

The optical bench is shown in the form of side and front elevations in Figure 8.2 and the scale of inches between the two will enable the dimensions to be determined. The dimensions shown can be followed exactly with advantage, as they have been worked out to give a bench of convenient smallness but with enough height to give adequate adjustment of the lamp-to-meter distance.

The bench is made of timber, and the main construction is of $\frac{1}{2}$ in. plywood which does not warp or twist. If the various parts can be cut on a circular saw, perfect squareness is assured, and it is worth seeking the co-operation of a do-it-yourself friend who has a small power saw.

The base of the bench is made of two pieces of $\frac{1}{2}$ in. ply, between which is sandwiched a sheet of thick metal to serve as a weight to prevent the bench being at all unstable. The author made use of an old copper half-tone block that

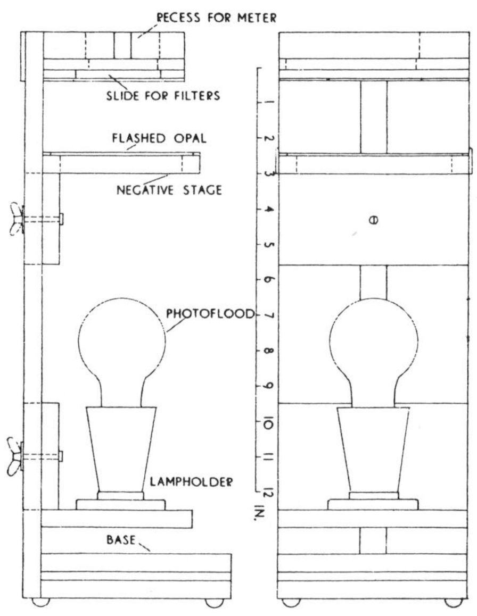

Fig. 8.2 Side and front elevations of the author's optical bench embodying an exposure meter. The scale of inches enables the dimensions to be copied exactly if desired.

served the purpose admirably. A $\frac{1}{4}$ in. hole was drilled in each of the four corners of the copper to accommodate the screws holding the two halves of the base together.

Two uprights, with a space of $\frac{3}{4}$ in. between them, form the runners to which are secured the meter-housing, the negative stage, and the lamp carriage. The meter-housing is permanently screwed to the top of the uprights, but the negative-stage and lamp carriage can be slid up and down and locked in position where required by means of a screw, large washer, and wingnut.

The uprights are held at the correct distance apart at the top by means of a thin plywood distance-piece. It is important that the space between the two uprights shall be exactly parallel, otherwise the two sliding portions of the bench will be alternately too loose and too tight.

The meter-housing, with which is combined the slide for the tricolour filters, consists of four layers of wood. The top one is $\frac{3}{4}$ in. thick and has a portion cut out exactly the same shape and size as the Weston meter. The original bench was designed for the Weston Master IV and V meters, but the cut-out portion can be made to suit any of the earlier versions. (Figure 8.3).

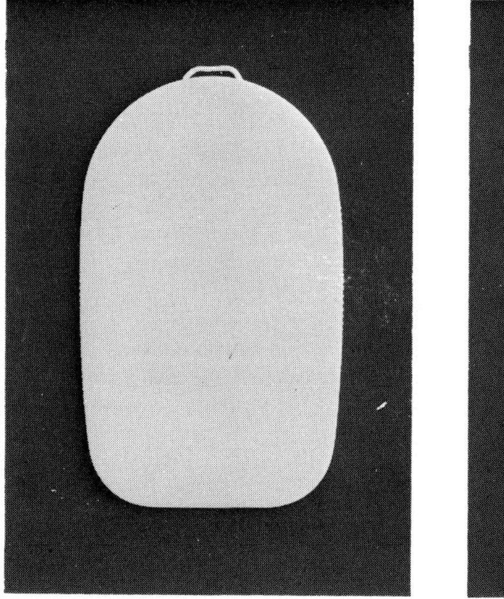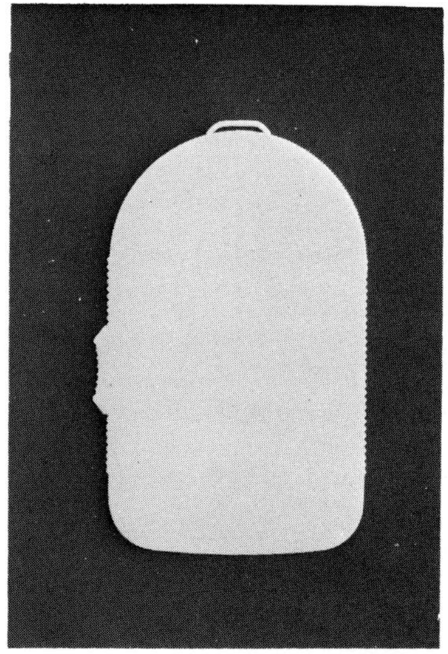

Fig. 8.3 Silhouettes of the Weston Master meters   II and III, and IV and V. These outlines should be followed in constructing the meter housing for the integrating photometer described. They are not actual size.

Immediately below the meter-housing is a layer of plywood with an aperture cut in it the shape of an hour-glass, corresponding to the cell window and the hinged baffle of the meter. The baffle is always in its open position in the optical bench, and so provision has to be made to accommodate it.

Below the meter is a slide $2\frac{1}{2}$ in. wide to take the tricolour filters, which are held between two pieces of card or thin plywood. A filter-holder just a little less than $2\frac{1}{2}$ in. wide permits the use of filter-apertures about 2 in. in diameter, which is big enough to cover the cell window amply without the position of the holder being too critical. Obviously the photocell must not be obstructed in any way while taking a reading, as this would give misleading results. The lowest layer of plywood is only $\frac{1}{16}$ in. thick as it has only to support the filters in their holder.

The negative stage is a frame of $\frac{1}{2}$ in. ply, the rectangular aperture in it being cut out with a coping saw or a fretsaw fitted with a toymaking blade. A narrow frame built up of two layers of $\frac{1}{16}$ in. ply, glued together and stuck on top of the stage, forms a recess $\frac{1}{8}$ in. deep to hold a sheet of flashed opal glass. The latter is obtainable quite cheaply from any large glass supplier and cut exactly to the size required.

The supporting bracket for the negative stage is of $\frac{1}{2}$ in. ply and is screwed to the stage as shown in Figure 8.2. A strip of $\frac{1}{2}$ in. ply, $\frac{3}{4}$ in. wide is screwed to the rear of the bracket and serves as a guide, working in the gap between the uprights.

The lamp-carriage is constructed in a similar manner to the negative stage, but no aperture is required in it. A batten bayonet lampholder is screwed to the carriage and is wired up with twin flex and a cord switch to a suitable plug. If the dimensions of Figure 8.2 are followed the lamp, negative stage, and meter cell window will all be accurately in line.

For negatives smaller than the size of the opal glass of the stage, glass mask-plates are used cut to exactly the same size as the top of the stage. The plates are masked down to size with lantern-slide binding-tape to slightly less than the dimensions of the image. For $2\frac{1}{4}$ in. square negatives, for example, a 2 in. square mask-aperture is suitable.

It is vital that none of the clear rebates of a negative shall be included in measurements, and it is wise, therefore, to use a smaller mask aperture. The sides of the negative stage are provided with slightly raised strips of thin ply, as shown in the diagram, to keep the mask-plate in position laterally.

To make sure that each filter is in exactly the correct position in front of the cell window "V" nicks are cut in the edge of the filter-holder in line with the centre of each gelatine, and a spring-loaded plywood plunger, operating in a channel in the side of the filter-slide, engages in the nicks as the holder is pushed through the slide.

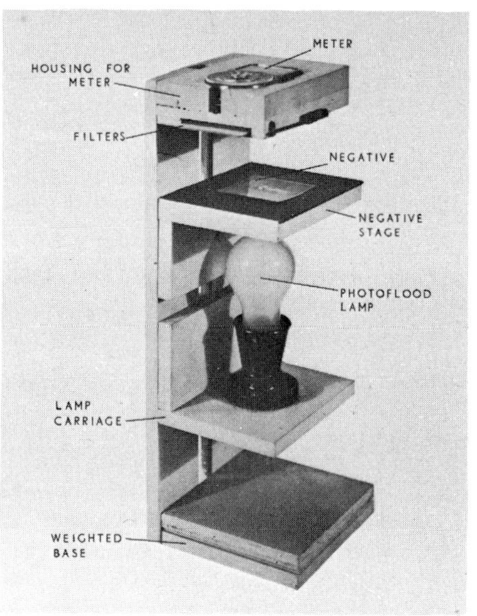

Fig. 8.4 Vertical optical bench to take a Weston Master exposure meter for use as an integrating enlarging photometer for off-easel negative evaluation. It is suitable for both monochrome and colour negatives.

The optimum distance between the meter-housing and the negative stage can be found experimentally by setting up the equipment so as to obtain a good needle deflection with no negative in place, and then moving a sheet of card across the stage starting at one edge. If the opal is too near the meter, so that the angle of acceptance is over-filled, the needle will not move until the card has covered quite a distance.

This is not a critical matter, but for the sake of efficiency the acceptance angle of the meter should be used fully. When measuring small negatives there is no need to alter the position of the stage, although obviously, in this case, the acceptance angle will not be filled. Some photographs of the author's optical bench are reproduced on pages 82, 83 and 84. These show some of the constructional details but there is no reason why these should not be modified to meet individual requirements and resources.

A front view of the instrument is shown in the photograph on this page, and the general arrangement of the lamp-carriage, negative-stage, and meter-housing can be seen. The

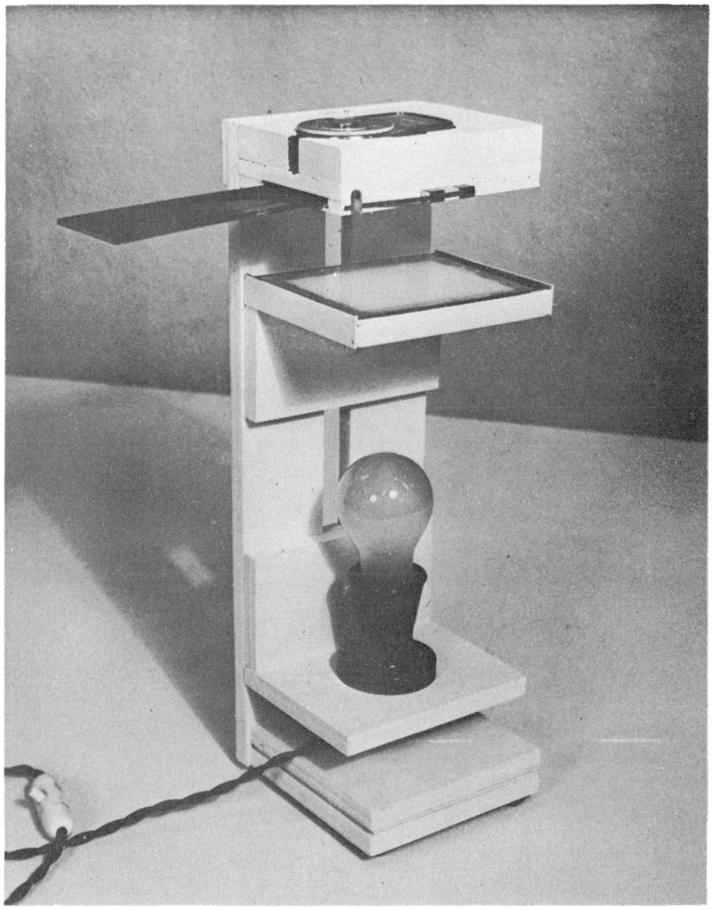

Fig. 8.5 Front view of optical bench for Weston Master meter. It shows the lamp carriage, negative stage and meter housing.

filter-holder carrying the appropriate tricolour filters can be seen protruding from its slide. Rubber feet were fixed to the underside of the base to prevent marking any furniture on which the instrument may be used, bearing in mind that measurements need not be carried out in the darkroom but may be disposed of in comfort by the fireside before starting a printing session.

A rear view of the bench is shown below and the method for sliding and locking the negative stage and lamp-carriage is made plain. The wooden strips on the rear of the

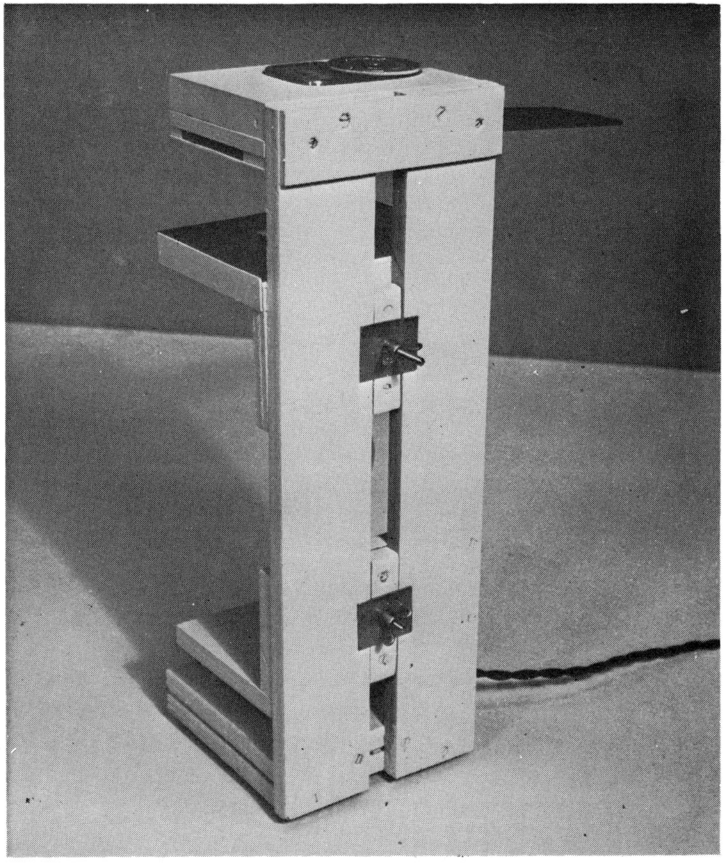

Fig. 8.6 Rear view of bench. Sliding adjustments of lamp carriage and negative stage with clamp plates and wing nuts can be seen.

brackets running in the space between the two uprights prevent the stage and carriage twisting as they are raised and lowered, and from this point of view the clearances should be kept to the bare minimum required for easy sliding.

Rectangular metal plates with a central hole were used instead of round washers for clamping the stage and lamp-carriage in any desired position. These give large pressure surfaces that are not likely to bruise the wooden uprights should the wingnuts be over-tightened. The wooden guide-strips should

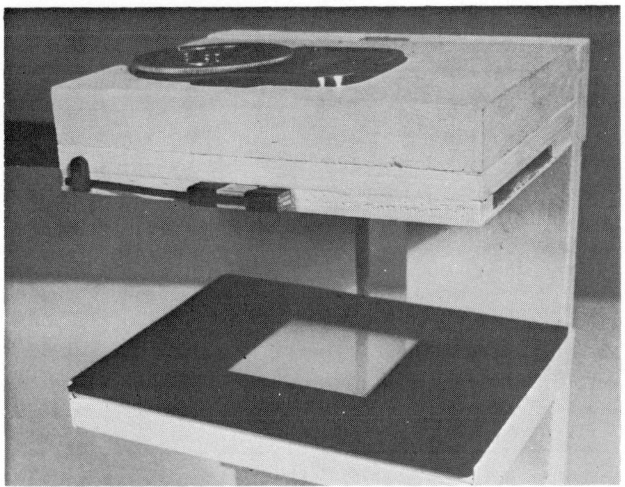

Fig. 8.7 Close-up of meter housing and negative stage. The spring-loaded plunger for accurate location of filters is shown and also the aperture to take the mounted filters.

be glasspapered vigorously on their rear surface to make them very slightly thinner than the uprights, otherwise the clamping nuts are likely to be ineffective.

When once the optimum position for the negative-stage has been found by experiment it is not likely that it will have to be moved again, except perhaps if the stage has to be removed from the bench for any reason. It is worth marking its position clearly so that it can be replaced there.

Figure 8.8 is a close-up of the negative-stage showing the flashed opal glass. This has strips of lantern-slide binding-tape on its lower surface along each edge to prevent white light being scattered around the edges of negatives. The heat from the lamp tends to dry out the gum on the masking strips, and the adhesion may deteriorate in time.

This can be seen in the photograph, where there are obvious pockets of air in places along the strips. Self-adhesive masking tape is unsatisfactory in this location, as the rather elevated temperature softens the adhesive layer and makes it tacky.

Details can be seen of the spring-loaded plunger that engages in V-shaped nicks in the edge of the filter-holder

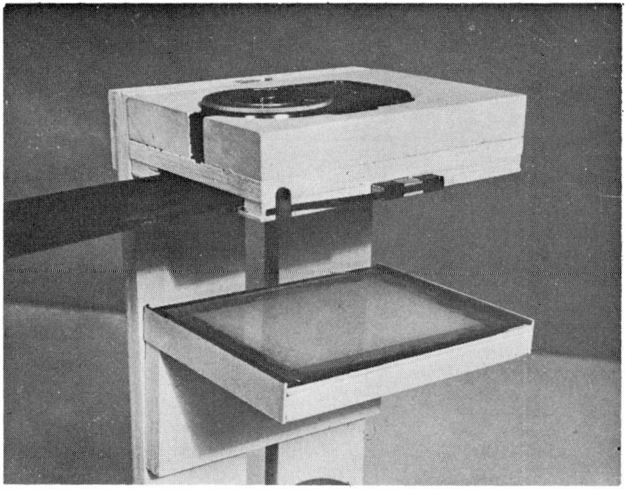

Fig. 8.8 Negative stage with opal glass. Smaller masks can be fitted to the stage as required.

to ensure correct location of each filter concentrically in front of the photocell window. The plunger is T-shaped, with its foot cut to a point to fit the nicks in the filter-slide. The spring-loading is provided by a 3 in. length of watch-spring secured to the top edge of the plunger with adhesive tape, and to the body of the meter-housing by means of half of the fibre cable-clamp from an old three-pin plug.

Quite accidentally, in the case of the bench illustrated, the plunger allows the filters to be pushed from right to left through their slide, but they cannot be withdrawn from left to right without withdrawing the plunger slightly. This proves a useful safeguard against removing the filters in error while the photoflood is switched on, — an accident that might damage the meter.

Further details of the plunger are shown in Figure 8.7, and a mask-plate for negatives smaller than the stage is shown in position between the guides on the two sides of the stage. The mask aperture is 2 in. square and is intended for $2\frac{1}{4}$ in. square negatives. The aperture is centred on the plate so that it is also centred with the lamp and cell.

When a mask-plate is in use, the meter is affected only by light coming through the negative in the aperture, as the surrounding black paper strips do not reflect a significant amount of light. It does not seem to matter if a negative curls a little as long as no unobscured opal is "seen" by the meter. Negatives that curl badly and obstinately just have to be kept flat with an additional sheet of clean glass placed on top of the film.

For measuring the densities of black and white negatives an ordinary 60-watt opal lamp is suitable. Alternatively, a 75-watt photo enlarger lamp is satisfactory. An opaque mask of black paper or thin metal is required for every size of negative as it is vital that no clear glass around the image of the negative shall be included in the measurements. To this end, the mask apertures must be slightly smaller than the image.

With no negative on the stage the lamp distance is adjusted so that the meter needle shows exactly full-scale deflection. It is necessary to have the baffle of the Weston Master meter in the open position so as to bring the low light scale into use. Full-scale needle deflection represents zero density and if a negative is now placed on the stage to cover the mask aperture, the needle deflection will be reduced and the reduction is a measure of the total density of the negative.

As the meter dial is scaled in light units (candelas per square foot) or arbitrary numbers, it is necessary to use suitable scale charts to convert meter readings into density values. Such a chart for the Weston Master V meter is reproduced in Figure 8.9, and it should be self-explanatory. It is convenient to drop the decimal points from the density values so that 0.1, 0.2 and 0.3 become 1, 2, and 3 respectively. In effect, the density readings are being multiplied by 10 which makes them more convenient and in this form they may be referred to as "negative indices". It will be shown later how negative indices may be used along with paper speed numbers and numbers related to the degree of enlargement, for arriving quickly at printing exposure times.

The total densities or indices of a large number of negatives can be measured in a very short time and they can be recorded, either in the margins of the negatives or on the filing envelopes.

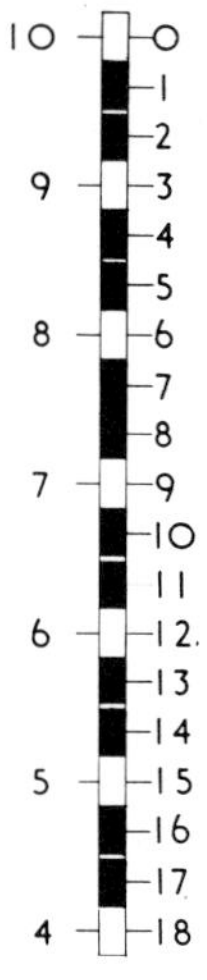

Fig. 8.9 Scale chart for Weston Master V meter when using it in an integrating photometer for printing black and white negatives.

Once measured and recorded they do not have to be measured again. Measurements can be carried out in normal room lighting but taking the precaution that no extraneous light enters the photocell window of the exposure meter. Check that, with the lamp switched off, the meter needle shows no deflection. An opaque card slipped momentarily in front of the cell window will show the smallest deflection resulting from any stray light. Nearby white walls should be avoided as they can bounce light from the densitometer lamp into the photocell window. With the lamp switched on and the masked aperture blanked out with black paper, the needle deflection should still be zero.

The printing exposure required is directly proportional

to the antilogarithm of the total density. Thus a negative with a total density of 0.6 calls for one-half the exposure required by a negative with a density of 0.9 the antilogarithms of these values being approximately 4 and 8 respectively. Those who are not at home with logarithms can take heart as there is no need to understand the theory of density measurements to make practical use of them although it does help in the solving of certain problems.

Measuring the total density of negatives in this way does not take into account any selective absorption of the silver deposit. The silver image of most negatives is free from colour due to developer stain, and modern fine-grain developers do not appear to produce the brownish images that were encountered with paraphenylene diamine. If, for any reason, a negative is brownish, it will absorb an unduly large amount of the blue light to which printing papers are mainly sensitive. Density measurements will not therefore be a reliable basis for exposure estimation.

This problem can be solved by inserting a suitable colour filter in the light beam of the densitometer. Ideally, such a filter should have a transmission that matches the spectral sensitivity of the printing paper which nowadays often extends into the blue-green region of the spectrum. A standard tri-colour blue filter such as the Wratten No. 47B has been found to be satisfactory with most papers. As this has a low transmission even in the blue region of the spectrum, the 60 or 75-watt lamp on the optical bench will have to be changed for a more powerful one. A No. 1 colour temperature controlled photoflood lamp will give adequate needle deflections with a strong blue filter in the light beam. With this arrangement it is feasible to determine printing exposures when making black and white enlargements from colour negatives on to blue-sensitive printing paper.

Off-easel evaluation of negatives, although much quicker than using an enlarger photometer in the darkroom, does not take into account the variations in exposure times made necessary by changes in the degree of enlargement. This has to be done separately but it can be carried out very quickly by scaling the enlarger with numbers that have been named "distance indices".

The relationship between the degree of enlargement and the exposure time required is not altogether a straightforward one. A simpler relationship can be found by regarding the enlarger lens as a point light source obeying the inverse square law of illumination. With a condenser and opal lamp enlarger, or one with a fully diffused illumination system, this law holds good.

The enlarger can be scaled with a logarithmic series of distance indices which.are related to the lens-to-paper distance in accordance with the formula —

$$\text{Distance index} = 20 \, \text{Log}_{10} \, d$$

where d is the lens-to-paper distance in inches (or centimetres if metric units are preferred).

In the table below are set out distance indices for lens-to-paper distances of from 4 to 40 inches, a range sufficient for most purposes. The indices have all been rounded off to the nearest one-half which represent an accuracy in calculated exposure times to within one-sixth of a lens stop.

Distance (in.)	Distance Index	Distance (in.)	Distance Index
4	12	24	$27\frac{1}{2}$
5	14	25	28
6	$15\frac{1}{2}$	26	28
7	17	27	$28\frac{1}{2}$
8	18	28	29
9	19	29	29
10	20	30	$29\frac{1}{2}$
11	21	31	30
12	$21\frac{1}{2}$	32	30
13	22	33	$30\frac{1}{2}$
14	23	34	$30\frac{1}{2}$
15	$23\frac{1}{2}$	35	31
16	24	36	31
17	$24\frac{1}{2}$	37	31
18	25	38	$31\frac{1}{2}$
19	$25\frac{1}{2}$	39	32
20	26	40	32
21	$26\frac{1}{2}$		
22	27		
23	27		

The numbers should be drawn legibly at intervals of 1 inch on a strip of white card. As legibility is important in the printing room it may be advisable to make use of transfer figures such as "Letraset" or "Driprint". The cardboard scale is fixed to the wall behind the enlarger taking care that the level of the iris diaphragm of the lens coincides with the lens-to-paper distance. Thus, when the lens is level with distance index 20 it should be at a distance of 10 inches from the surface of the easel. It is helpful to have a light-weight but rigid pointer attached to the lens panel so that its free end comes within a fraction of an inch of the scale on the wall. Distance indices can then be read off at a glance without pause during an enlarging session.

If the enlarger is of a type where the column is a sloping one, or the up and down movement of the enlarger head involves parallelogram levers, a pointer on the lens panel is of little value and a simple optical sighting device will have to be used instead. This can be contrived from brass wire or sheet metal.

In arriving at the correct printing exposure there are three main variables to take into account — negative index, distance index and paper speed index (See Chapter Nine on the speeds of printing paper). As all these values are logarithmic they can be added and subtracted instead of being multiplied or divided and, in use, the negative and distance indices are added together and the paper speed index subtracted from the total. The remainder or "final index" is used in conjunction with a simple table or calculator to arrive at the exposure time required. This procedure may seem to be unduly complicated but, in practice, it is quicker than using a photometer on the enlarger easel.

The f/number at which the exposure is made is an additional factor affecting exposure but it is convenient to work out all exposures for the smallest aperture of the lens and then to open up the stop, click by click, to bring the time to convenient shortness. Thus, if the exposure works out to be 200 seconds at f/22, then it is 100 seconds at f/16, 50 seconds at f/11, 25 seconds at f/8 and 12½ seconds at f/5.6. The last time is conveniently short but it is long enough to permit any dodging to be carried out.

When setting up any system of printing exposure estimation based on measurement the starting point has to be the making of a good straight print from a "standard" negative arriving at the correct exposure time by the usual trial and error methods. For this important trial print it is essential to give a median time of development (say 2 minutes) in fresh

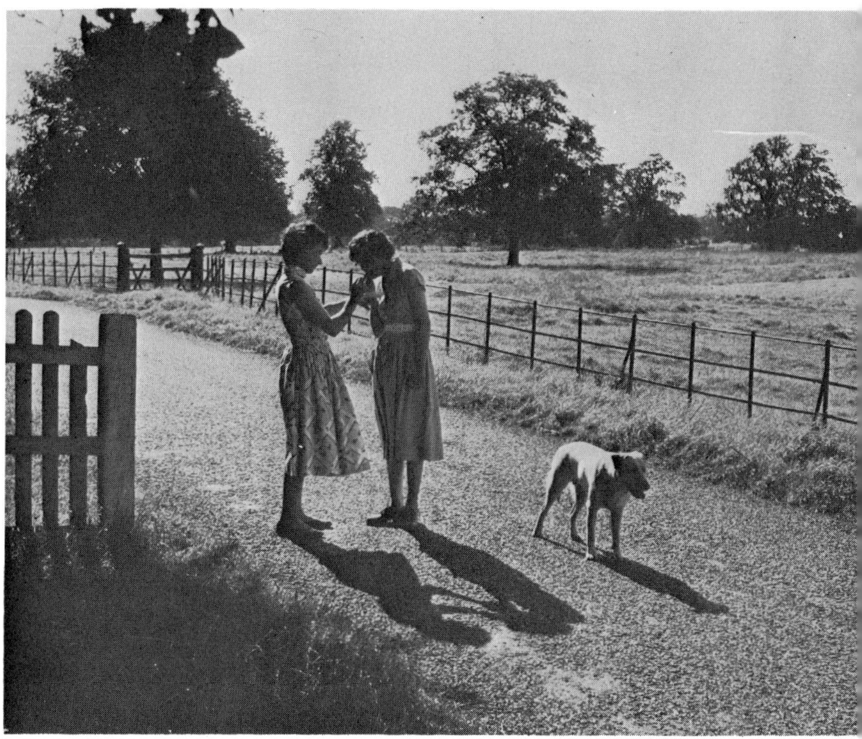

Fig. 8.10 The author's standard negative. It is many years old as can be seen from the fashions but it is a good standard as the actual value of $\Delta\overline{D}$ is the same as the theoretical value (0.39). The negative index is 6½.

developer adjusted to the normal working temperature of 68° F. It is important too that the contrast of the negative chosen as a standard shall exactly suit the photographer's usual normal grade of paper. Also, for convenience in constructing the final exposure table or calculator, the smallest lens aperture of the enlarger lens — probably f/22 — should be used for making the reference print. Printing papers suffer from low-intensity reciprocity failure which means, in effect, that they are slower at long exposure times than at short. A small degree of enlargement should be employed for making the initial trial print so that, even at f/22, the exposure time required is of the order of 10 seconds. If the trial print requires an exposure time of say 100 seconds the resulting table or calculator will be misleading as printing exposures in practice are usually no longer than about 20 seconds.

Setting up a system of exposure estimation using an integrating measurement method calls for a rather special standard negative. It should have a well-balanced density distribution with no very large highlights or shadows. The aim, in fact, is to find a negative of which the actual value of $\Delta \overline{D}$ is as close as possible to the theoretical value. The author was able to find such a negative and a print from it is reproduced on page 92. It should not be concluded that this is a linear negative just because of close agreement between the actual and theoretical values of $\Delta \overline{D}$. It serves the same purpose however in this context. It is sufficient to select a standard negative visually as unbalanced density distribution is usually very obvious.

Having made a satisfactory trial print from a standard negative under carefully controlled conditions, it may be found, for example, that a negative with an index of 6 and the enlarger set at a distance index of 20 (10 in. between lens and printing paper) gives a print of suitable depth with an exposure of 10 seconds at f/22. This is all the information that is needed for working out exposure times for other negatives and degrees of enlargement. If the negative index (6) is added to the distance index (20) we have a total of 26. Assuming a normal grade of paper with a speed index of 10°, this is subtracted from 26 giving a remainder of 16. This is the "final index" referred to earlier.

Assuming that the preliminary test print was given an exposure time of 10 seconds at f/22 we have the situation that a final index of 16 is equivalent to an exposure time of 10 seconds and from this information the complete exposure table can be compiled, thus —

Final Index	Exposure Time (Seconds)
10	$2\frac{1}{2}$
11	3
12	4
13	5
14	6
15	8
16	10
17	12
18	16
19	20
20	25
21	32
22	40
23	50
24	64
25	80
26	100
27	128
28	160
29	200
30	250
31	320
32	400

It will be realised that as the final indices are logarithmic, the series of exposure times are in geometric progression with a common ration of $\sqrt[3]{2}$, or 1.26. For final indices that include one-half, viz. $20\frac{1}{2}$, the appropriate exposure time is found by interpolation, in this case between 25 and 32 seconds.

The exposure table can be made in the form of a sliding calculator as illustrated in Figure 8.11. It is then possible to adjust the general level of exposure times by intervals of one-third of a stop. This may be necessary as the enlarger lamp slowly ages and its light emission falls. There comes the time when all prints have to be developed for a little longer than the standard 2 minutes, an indication of slight under-exposure. By shifting the two scales of the calculator relative to each other to increase all exposure times by one-third of a stop the loss of light from the lamp is compensated for. Eventually, the enlarger lamp fails and has to be replaced by a new one. When this happens the calculator has to be set back to its previous position or even to one-third of a stop less exposure than initially.

It may be wondered why it has been suggested that the exposure table be based on a lens aperture of f/22. There are two important reasons for this; firstly it enables awkward

FINAL INDEX	SECONDS
10	2-1/2
11	3
12	4
13	5
14	6
15	8
16	10
17	12
18	16
19	20
20	25
21	32
22	40
23	50
24	64
25	80
26	100
27	125
28	160
29	200
30	250
31	320
32	400
33	500

Fig. 8.11 Simple sliding calculator for exposure determination when using the home-made integrating photometer described in the text.

fractions of a second to be avoided in the series of exposure times at small values of the final index on the exposure calculator. Secondly, the series of f/numbers on some enlarger lenses have an odd interval between the largest aperture and the next, e.g. f/4.5 and f/5.6. Stopping down from f/4.5 to f/5.6 involves increasing the exposure time by a factor of about 1½ instead of 2 which is the normal factor for f/numbers. By working from f/22 this odd interval is avoided except on the very rare occasions when it is necessary to expose at full aperture.

As modern enlarging lenses are fitted with click stops there is no difficulty in finding the correct exposing aperture without having to peer at a scale of numbers. It cannot be claimed that click stops are always accurately calibrated but any errors are generally small enough to be of no significance in practical work.

While the optical bench incorporating an exposure meter can be used for all negative sizes it is perhaps not ideal for 35 mm and half-frame negatives. Lengths of film are not easy to manipulate without scratching them and a specially constructed densitometer for measuring total densities of strips of 35 mm negatives is worth constructing. Such a device can be used also for evaluating colour transparencies from which it is proposed to make black and white negatives and from this it is but a short step to the evaluation of 35 mm colour negatives for colour printing.

The construction of such a densitometer is made easier by the availability of a suitable selenium photocell made in Japan and selling at about 25 pence. The author has such a cell which is rectangular in shape and having an active area almost exactly 24 x 36 mm. Its overall size is about $1\frac{1}{2}$ x $1\frac{1}{8}$ in. The cell is more than sensitive enough for this

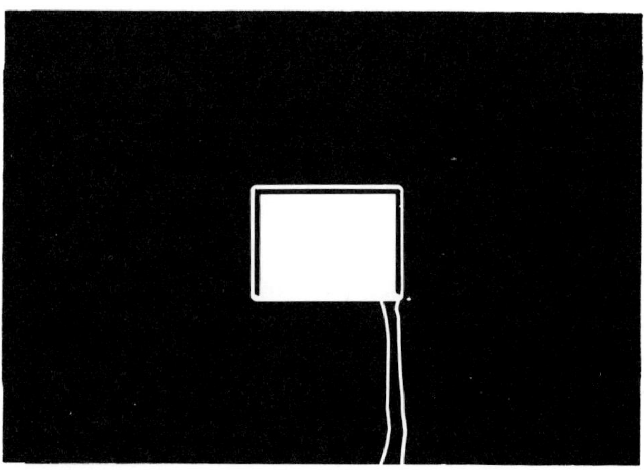

Fig. 8.12 Shadowgraph of selenium cell roughly the same size as a 35mm negative (24 x 36mm). This particular cell is of Japanese manufacture and cost 25 pence.

present purpose and has an output of roughly 750 micro-amperes when illuminated with a 60-watt lamp 4 in. away. Messrs. Proops Ltd., of Tottenham Court Road, London, supply such cells and they are provided with thin flexible leads for connection purposes.

The only essential component apart from the cell is a microammeter and a suitable instrument may be found among ex-Government surplus equipment for a few shillings. The range is not important but the physical length of the scale should be as big as can be found for the sake of reading accuracy.

The relationship between the light falling on the cell and the needle deflection obtained depends on the resistance of the external circuit. If the cell is connected directly to a meter having a coil resistance of only a few hundred ohms, the reading is likely to be directly proportional to the light falling on the cell. This can be checked quite easily by placing the cell in the illuminated area provided by the enlarger lens and using the click stops of the lens to obtain a series of illuminations differing by a factor of two. To obtain the biggest possible needle deflection with the lens

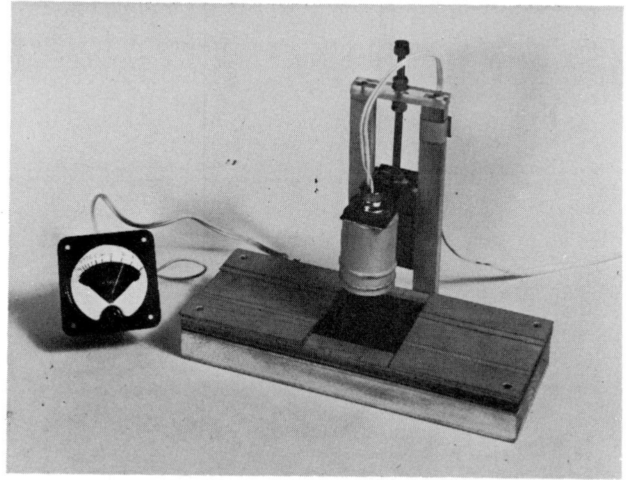

Fig. 8.13 Hooked-up integrating photometer for 35 mm negatives embodying a rectangular selenium photocell and a small microammeter bought for 12½ pence at a junk shop. A small 12-volt lamp was used, operated via a transformer.

wide open it may be necessary to bring the enlarger right to the bottom of its column. It is necessary also to check that all the aperture intervals are one stop; on many lenses there is a series of f/numbers that runs: f/4.5, f/5.6, f/8, f/11, f/16 and f/22. Of these the first two numbers do not represent a one-stop interval and in such cases the largest aperture has to be avoided.

An arithmetic scale is not ideal for any kind of exposure meter and by inserting a resistance of suitable value in series with the photocell and meter a nearly logarithmic scale may be obtained. A wire-wound volume control of about 10,000 ohms can be used for determining the optimum value of the series resistance. It can then either be replaced with a fixed resistor or the potentiometer can be locked so that it cannot be altered inadvertently. It has been found that with a 60-watt opal lamp about 6 in. above the cell full-scale needle deflection (50 microamps) could be obtained with about 2,500 ohms in series. When the light on the cell was reduced by steps of X2, the following readings were obtained: 50, 47, 44, 40, 35, 26, and 18. This is a range of six stops and a further stop could have been obtained at the lower end had means been available for reducing the light further. With an arithmetic scale such as results when the cell is connected directly to the meter, the readings were 50, 25, $12\frac{1}{2}$, $6\frac{1}{4}$ and 3. This is a range of four stops only and it would not be feasible to squeeze in another.

The actual design of the densitometer can be made to suit individual requirements but it is desirable to divorce negative measurement from the enlarger baseboard for the sake of good working illumination for reading the scale of the meter. A possible arrangement is shown in Figure 8.14 the lower section of the diagram being a plan view of the working top with the recessed photocell and a suitable channel in which a length of 35 mm negatives may be laid without risk of scratches.

Plywood of various thicknesses down to 1 mm is excellent material for building this type of equipment and the thinner plys can be cut with a craft knife. The cell itself should be recessed and its surface protected with a thin cover glass, the latter carrying an opaque mask with an aperture slightly smaller than 24 x 36 mm to ensure that only the images of negatives and not the rebates are included in the measurements.

A column, adjustable in height, carries a batten-mounting lampholder to take a 60-watt opal lamp. Although not shown in the diagram, this can be fitted with a shade in the form of a cylinder — a suitable empty tin will serve — so that direct light from the source does not dazzle the operator. The suggested lamp is powerful enough for black and white

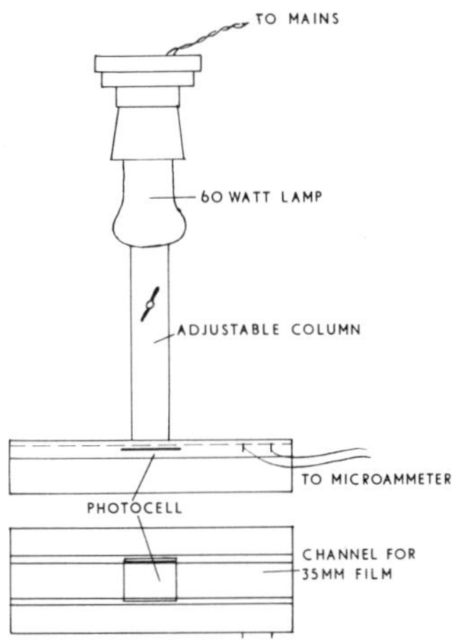

Fig. 8.14 Front elevation and plan of integrating densitometer utilising a rectangular selenium photocell and an external microammeter. This is designed for off-easel evaluation of 35mm negatives.

negative assessment but more light may be required for the evaluation of colour negatives.

The height of the lamp above the cell and the value of any series resistor employed determine the needle deflections obtained and the aim should be to secure full-scale needle deflection with no negative in front of the cell. This forms a reference point to which the needle can always be brought before beginning a series of readings. The adjustment of the height of the lamp allows this to be done.

There now arises the problem of calibrating the instrument and the use of the click stops on an enlarger lens is not very satisfactory even if the illumination level on the cell can be made high enough. What is needed is the equivalent of a series of calibrated neutral density filters that can be laid in turn over the cell and the microammeter readings noted.

It has been found possible to make the equivalent of a series of such filters in the following manner. On a sheet of centimetre graph paper with pale blue lines a chess board pattern is drawn in indian ink with the squares having 0.5 cm sides. The area of the pattern should be about 4 x 5 in. and if this is imagined to be a line image on film it is apparent that the light transmission will be 50 per cent, equivalent to a density of 0.3.

On the graph paper a section of the pattern about $1\frac{3}{4}$ in. x $1\frac{1}{2}$ in. is left as it is as black and white squares. The remainder now has half of each white square blackened out and a similar size of pattern is left like this. All the white triangles elsewhere have half their areas blackened and the process is continued until there are six sections in all with progressively smaller areas of white producing the equivalent of a series of densities of 0.3, 0.6, 0.9, 1.2, 1.5 and 1.8.

A contact line negative is made by transmission copying and a line positive on film made from the negative. The positive should be treated in dilute Farmer's reducer to make sure there is no development fog. The several sections of the positive may be laid in turn over the photocell and the meter calibrated at one-stop intervals. A proper scale can be drawn on a piece of clear film and this fitted to the glass of the microammeter. Calibration at one-third of a stop intervals can be carried out by interpolation.

The pattern shown in Figure 8.15 was drawn freehand with a brush but despite its crudity it proved surprisingly accurate for this present purpose. Figure 8.16 shows in detail how the pattern is constructed.

If the microammeter is calibrated over as wide a range as possible at one-third of a stop intervals the marks on the added scale can be assigned suitable numbers. It is logical to make full-scale needle deflection zero and to number the other marks, 1, 2, 3, 4, and so on. A difference of 1 in the reading of a negative means an exposure difference of one-third of a stop.

In describing this simple photocell and microammeter device

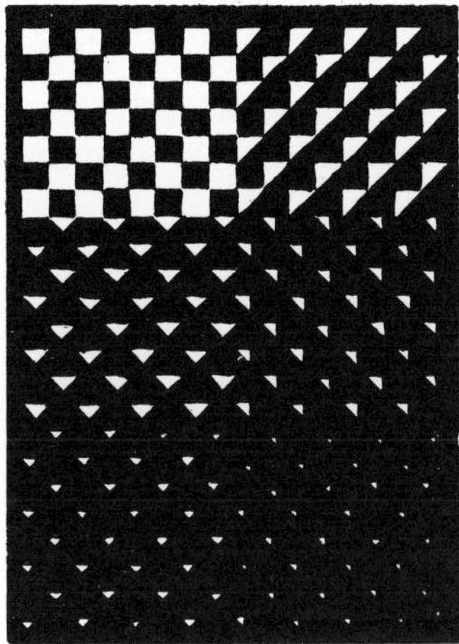

Fig. 8.15 The black and white geometric pattern described in the text used as a basis for a series of neutral density filters for calibrating an enlarging photometer.

Fig. 8.16 Details of the geometric pattern shown in Figure 8.15.

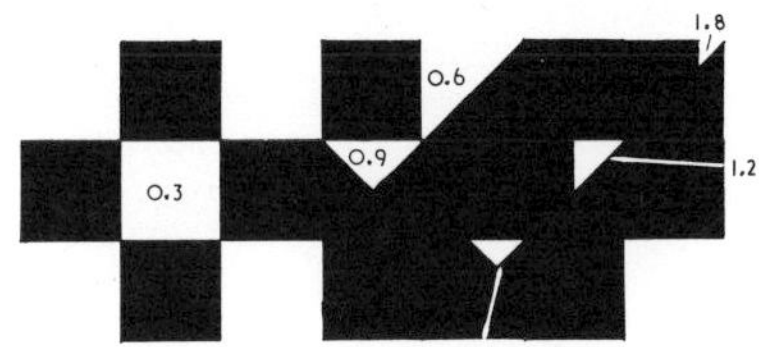

for the evaluation of 35 mm negatives in strips some suggestions were made regarding the initial calibration of the instrument. This is necessary because the relationship between the light falling on the photocell and the readings given by the microammeter is not a linear one if a series resistor is included in the circuit. A linear relationship is obtained only if the resistance of the external circuit is low compared with that of the photocell.

A typical example is a cell and microammeter combination that calls for a scries resistor of about 2,500 ohms to produce a nearly logarithmic scale which is the ideal in this kind of device. However carefully the resistor is chosen by trial and error the resulting scale will be a little compressed at the top and bottom ends but this is not very important.

Using the series of neutral density filters in the form of black-and-white patterns described, the calibration procedure is very simple. The lamp should be positioned at a distance from the cell so that full-scale needle deflection is obtained with nothing in front of the cell. It is advisable to watch out for drift in the cell by leaving the lamp on for a minute or so when full-scale deflection has been established to make sure that it does not alter. The drift of a good cell is small but it can be either positive or negative, an increase or a decrease in needle deflection with time.

By placing the neutral density filters in turn over the cell and noting the readings a series of current values is obtained, each value corresponding to a particular density in front of the cell. The reading-density relationship for the author's cell and meter is shown in Figure 8.17, and the curve is rather like the characteristic curve of a high contrast reversal material

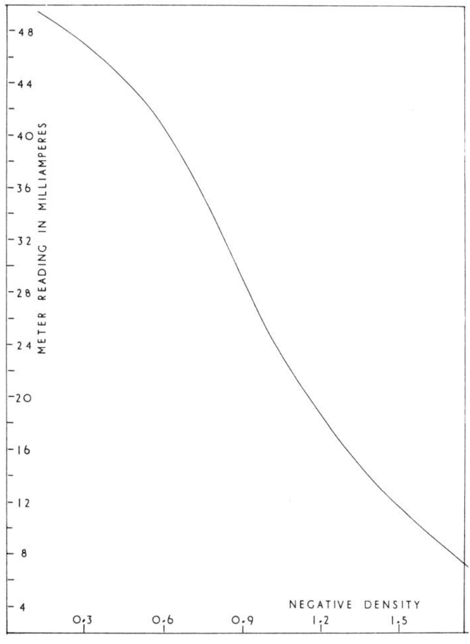

Fig. 8.17 The meter-reading/density relationship for a typical selenium cell and microammeter with a series resistor of several thousand ohms.

in that it has a toe and a shoulder and a region which is more or less straight. From such a graph it is possible to interpolate meter readings for density intervals of 0.1 and it is then a matter of making an additional scale for the microammeter for assigning to each negative measured a number related to density which can be called the "negative index". The only reason for abandoning actual density values is to avoid the decimal point that can so easily lead to error in hasty arithmetic.

Before considering the construction of a supplementary meter scale it is worth examining alternative methods of calibrating the meter. It is not essential to use a series of neutral density filters: one having a density of 0.3 is enough provided the distance between the lamp and the photocell is adjustable over a fairly wide range. The procedure is now as follows: the lamp distance is again adjusted to produce full-scale deflection and the 0.3 filter is placed over the cell. This will reduce the reading on the meter from, say 50 to 45 which should be noted. The filter is now removed from in front of the cell and the lamp distance increased until the meter needle is at 45 once more. The 0.3 filter is placed over the cell again and the reading again noted and with the filter removed the lamp is pulled farther away until this same reading is obtained. This continues until a sufficiently lengthy scale has been calibrated.

This simpler method has one obvious shortcoming. If the neutral density filter has an actual value departing significantly from its nominal value of 0.3 the error will accumulate so that the overall scale error can be quite big. The chessboard pattern suggested for making a 0.3 filter has been found to be satisfactorily accurate provided it is drawn with reasonable care. It has proved to be more accurate if drawn freehand with a brush because if it is ruled in the first instance and the black squares filled in with a brush the thickness of the ruled lines can introduce a small error. In any case, the lines should be kept extremely thin.

For checking the accuracy of the chessboard filter a line positive was made from a single-line photomechanical screen which is ruled very accurately with black lines on a clear ground, the spaces between the lines being equal to their width. It was found that in making the positive the exposure had to be kept to a minimum consistent with good opacity of the blacks otherwise irradiation increased the width of the lines at the expense of the clear spaces. Comparing such a neutral density filter with the chessboard pattern revealed that they were in very close agreement.

In Figure 8.18 is shown the microammeter scale to which has been added a scale of negative indices from 0 to 18. It will be noticed that the zero corresponds with the full-scale deflection of the microammeter. Figure 8.19 shows the part of the scale that is required for adding to the microammeter in the form of a sheet of clear film that can be affixed to the glass of the meter, taking care to position it correctly. The rest of the scale showing subdivisions and microampere values is already on the meter dial and it would be confusing to duplicate it on the glass.

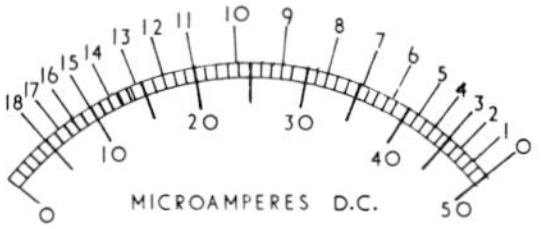

Fig. 8.18 Microammeter scale to which has been added an additional scale of negative indices, the latter having been determined from the graph in Figure 8.17.

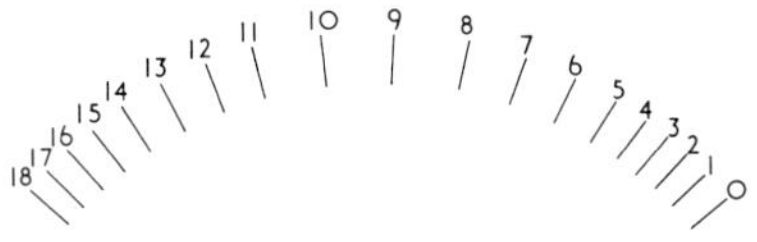

Fig. 8.19 Scale of negative indices that, in the form of a film positive, can be added to a microammeter by attaching it to the glass front.

With the scale shown in the diagrams it is possible to read negative densities to the nearest one-half without any trouble. A reading accuracy any better than this is pointless; a reading to the nearest one-half is equivalent to working to the nearest one-sixth of a stop as regards exposure.

The sensitive long-range CdS photometer described in Chapter 6 lends itself very well to on-easel measurement of the total light transmittance of negatives, the photocell being built into the enlarger baseboard or into a paper holder masking board. There is a very simple method whereby very high sensitivity may be obtained by optical means.

The latter are shown in section in Figure 8.20 and have to be let into the enlarger baseboard or into the masking board. A $2\frac{1}{2}$ in. diameter bi-convex lens with a focal length of 5 cm (obtainable from laboratory equipment suppliers such as Griffin and George Ltd.) is supported on a small handbag

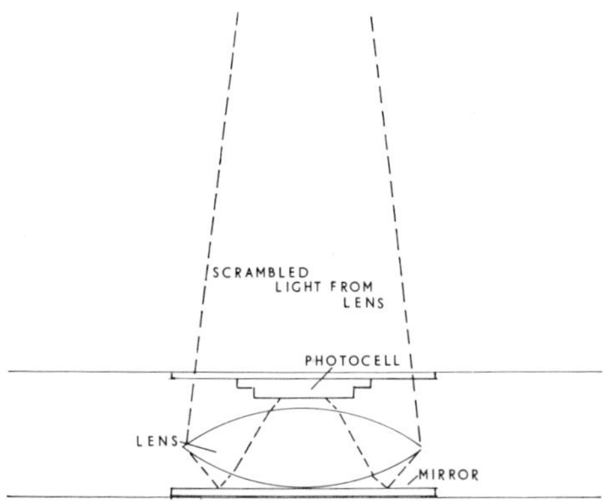

Fig. 8.20 Sectional view of the light-collecting system and CdS photo-cell that can be let into the enlarger baseboard or paper holder.

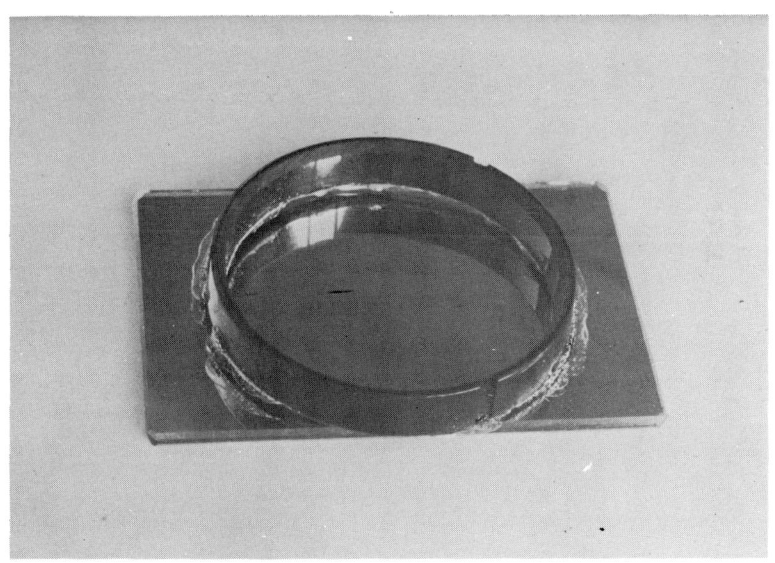

Fig. 8.21 Handbag mirror with plastic ring cemented to it for supporting a bi-convex lens.

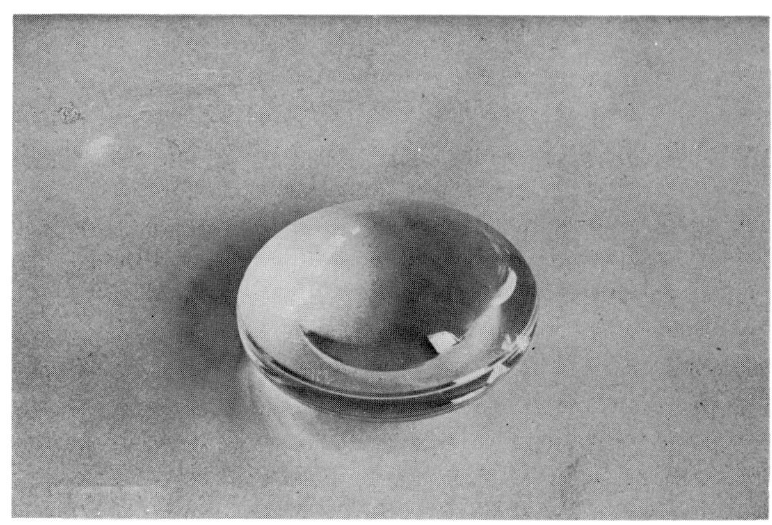

Fig. 8.22 Bi-convex lens to serve as a light collector and having a focal length of 5cm.

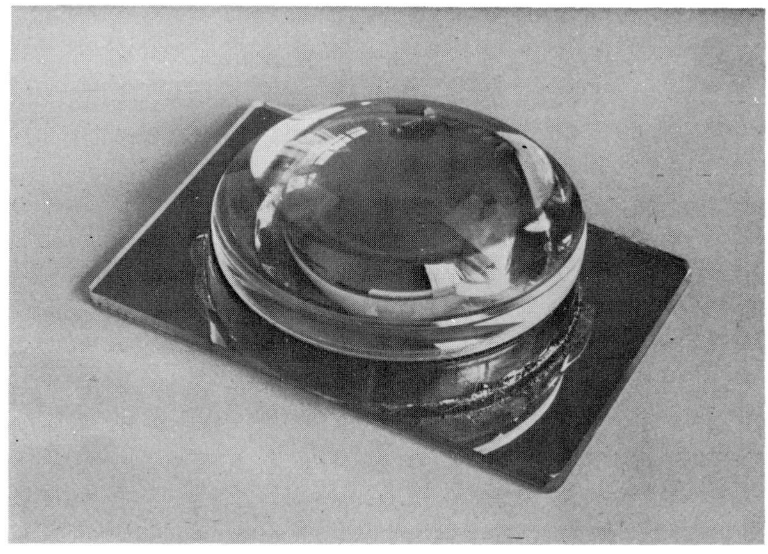

Fig. 8.23 Lens in position on the handbag mirror.

mirror by means of a plastic or metal ring. Light from the enlarger lens falls on the lens, is reflected back by the mirror through the lens again and is brought roughly to focus on the CdS cell which is supported, face down, just above the lens. The overall focal length of the system is 1 in. as the single lens is involved twice.

A scrambler of translucent plastic is placed in front of the enlarger lens while measurements are being taken so as to give an assessment of the total density of the negative. The photocell used was 1 in. in diameter. A cell of fair size is needed as the light from the lens is not brought to a point and it cannot be guaranteed that the enlarger lens is always accurately centred with the photocell collecting lens.

This optical arrangement has the additional advantage that the cell is not much affected by the safelighting unless this happens to be located directly above the enlarger. Oblique rays going through the photocell lens will not be focussed on the cell. It has been found that there is no need to switch off safelights while measuring but this point should be checked for individual conditions.

There is no need to cut à hole in the enlarger easel or masking board to try this system out. The optics can be set up on a handbag mirror, sticking the ring in place with polystyrene cement and seating the lens in the ring. A piece of thin plywood with side members to hold the mirror in position and to support the cell on stiff connecting wires is all that is required for preliminary tests.

It had been intended to build the microammeter and associated electronics into a masking frame; this was decided against on the grounds that the microammeter unit might have other uses apart from in the darkroom. The microammeter (0 to 50 microamperes) was therefore mounted on the sloping face of a portable wooden cabinet along with a pair of sockets into which the CdS leads are plugged. A small on-off switch for the range shift is also mounted on the panel and a double-pole on-off switch for the photocell circuit. The second pole of this switch is used to control a 1.25-volt M.E.S. lamp powered by a single U2 dry cell. This lamp, well shaded, illuminates the dial of the microammeter and serves also as a pilot light to indicate that the cell is switched on.

Inside the cabinet is housed the dry cell for the pilot light secured in a large tool clip. A plastic tube with connections to take up to three 1.34-volt mercury cells is also accommodated in a spring clip. The higher the working voltage the bigger the current for a given light level and it has been found that three cells — about 4 volts — are enough for the purpose. The three variable resistors in the form of potentiometers from ancient radio and television receivers are mounted on a strip of thick brass fixed towards the rear of the cabinet and drilled with $\frac{3}{8}$ in. holes to take the shanks of the potentiometers. The latter may be fitted with knobs or screwdriver slots for adjustment purposes.

The hooked-up circuit arrangement utilizing a light-collecting lens can be calibrated and tested before making it into any kind of permanent installation. Details of the simple optical system are shown in the accompanying photographs and it can be cleaned up when it has been made to work satisfactorily. It is worth mentioning that a concave mirror can be used in place of the bi-convex lens suggested and shown in the illustrations. For example, the plated metal reflector from an old cycle lamp or the rear-silvered mirror from an old-fashioned slide projector can be tried. In general, the focal length of such a mirror system is likely to be longer than that of a lens if only because the light goes twice through the lens whereas a mirror is involved only once. This is not a serious disadvantage if one is prepared to raise the enlarger baseboard by fitting it with rather long rubber feet so that the optical system can be accommodated in a square or circular aperture cut in the centre of the board. The diameter of the mirror, like that of a lens, governs the light-collecting ability for a given focal length and $2\frac{1}{2}$ to 3 in. is a suitable size.

It was suggested that a switched shunt be included in the microammeter circuit so that the range of the meter is extended by a factor of the order of 10. If a variable resistor is fitted it is a simple matter to arrive at the correct setting for any required range shift. If an illumination is allowed to fall on the cell so that full-scale deflection is obtained exactly, the necessary adjustments can be carried out easily. If a thin negative is focused to, say 3-diameters and the lens stopped down to f/5.6, we have the maximum light conditions likely to be encountered in practical photometry. A scrambler of frosted plastic or ground glass is positioned in front of the lens and the light is now equivalent to that calling for very short exposures of less than one second's duration.

Before switching on the photometer under these conditions it is essential to see that the shunt is in circuit. Without it there is considerable risk of damage to the sensitive moving coil mechanism. When the preliminary adjustments have been effected, it is worth substituting a "press-to-open" switch for the conventional on-off switch in the shunt circuit. Such a spring-loaded switch ensures that the shunt is always across the meter unless the finger is pressing the button. Alternatively, it may be possible to fit a light spring to the toggle of a conventional switch so that it always returns to the "on" position when it is released.

The calibration of the meter dial can take any form that is convenient for the user. It can be directly in exposure times for say a normal grade of·paper, exposure times for other grades being worked out on the basis of their relative mid-tone speeds. Alternatively, the calibration can be in the form of an arbitrary scale of numbers, a difference of 1 being equivalent to one-third of a stop. This ties up with the suggested system for the densitometer embodying a Weston meter and the general level of the numbers can be fixed so that, by subtracting the appropriate paper speed index from the meter reading, the remainder can be used in conjunction with a table or calculator for arriving at the exposure time.

Provided the electronic circuitry is wired to ensure low resistance connections by using soldered joints wherever practicable, the photometer will give very consistent results over long periods. The mercury batteries maintain their voltage during most of their life and should last at least twelve months. Care in calibration is repaid in the form of accurate exposure indications. These will naturally be based on photographic tests, all trial exposures being developed for a standard time at 68° F. in the printing paper developer normally used. As the photometer measures essentially the total density of the negative, corrections of half-a-stop should be made for negatives having obviously large shadows or unduly large highlights. A vital precaution is to use an opaque mask in the negative carrier and not a red celluloid one, and the mask opening must be kept always the same when taking photometer readings. No clear rebates of negatives must be included in the masked area.

There is an alternative method of range-shifting that enables a single additional scale to be used. This is an optical method involving a suitable neutral density filter that can be placed in the light path or removed as required. A density of 1.0 is convenient and it will be found that the same series of meter readings will be obtained at different f/numbers when the N.D. filter is removed as when it is in position. The solid curves in Figure 5.17 illustrate this point.

If a scale is drawn for the meter giving exposure times arrived at with the filter in the light path, the readings have merely to be multiplied by 10 when measurements of low light levels are made with the N.D. filter pulled out of the light path. It is practicable to arrange a spring-loaded mechanism so that the N.D. filter is always in the light path until it is deliberately removed by means of a lever or cord just to take a reading.

A neutral density filter 2 in. square now costs about a pound and in ordering one the density required — 1.0 in this case must be specified. The collecting lens the author used was of such a diameter that an N.D. filter 3 in. square was required and this costs over two pounds. Unfortunately, a piece of fogged film of the correct density will not do in this situation as the silver deposit scatters light. It might be worth staining fixed-out and washed film in diluted black retouching dye, achieving the correct density by trial and error. The density can be measured accurately enough for the present purpose by using a densitometer that utilizes a Weston meter. Dyed films should be measured when dry as they change density somewhat on drying.

As a good masking board for the enlarger easel is expensive and as cheap ones are invariably flimsy and inaccurate, it is worth making one and incorporating the CdS photometer optical system as suggested earlier. This can be done very successfully. It was decided that, as flush-mounting of prints is becoming so widespread, white borders are not always desirable as they are trimmed off, making a 10 x 12 in. print a mere $9\frac{1}{2}$ in. x $11\frac{1}{2}$ in. Without masking blades the printing paper has to be held flat on the easel by means which do not encroach unduly into the picture area, and four small button magnets in conjunction with a sheet of tinplate in the easel are ideal as they can be used to nip the extreme corners of the paper and will hold even double-weight material firmly.

This feature was built into the home-made paper-holder, the top surface of which consists of a sheet of $\frac{1}{4}$ in. plywood on top of which is cemented a sheet of tinplate. Onto the tinplate is stretched some white Fablon, a material widely used for covering kitchen working tops and having an adhesive back. Masking facilities are provided for making prints that require white borders but the masking blades can be discarded completely when they are not in use.

A circular aperture, $2\frac{1}{2}$ in. in diameter, in the surface of the paper-holder allows scrambled light from the enlarger lens to fall on the CdS cell assembly. A $3\frac{1}{4}$ in. square lantern slide cover glass inset into the plywood protects the optical system from dust. The connections from the photocell are taken to a socket let into one side or the rear of the frame of the paper-holder and a plug into this enables the cell to be linked with the associated battery and microammeter. The circuit of the latter, being independent of the optical system, can be changed as desired with the developments in electronics without the need for changing the construction of the paper-holder.

The basis of the holder is a frame of 2 x 1 in. hardwood battens measuring 18 x 22 in. This size enables masked prints up to 12 x 15 in. to be made and unmasked prints up to 16 x 20 in. The corners of the frame are mitred and are glued and screwed, and the assembly must be perfectly flat so that it cannot rock on the enlarger easel. To this end it should be checked during assembly by placing it on a perfectly plane surface. Two battens, 1 x $1\frac{3}{4}$ in., are positioned across the frame; these are to support the mirror and photo-cell on a metal plate screwed to the battens as shown in the photographs on page 113.

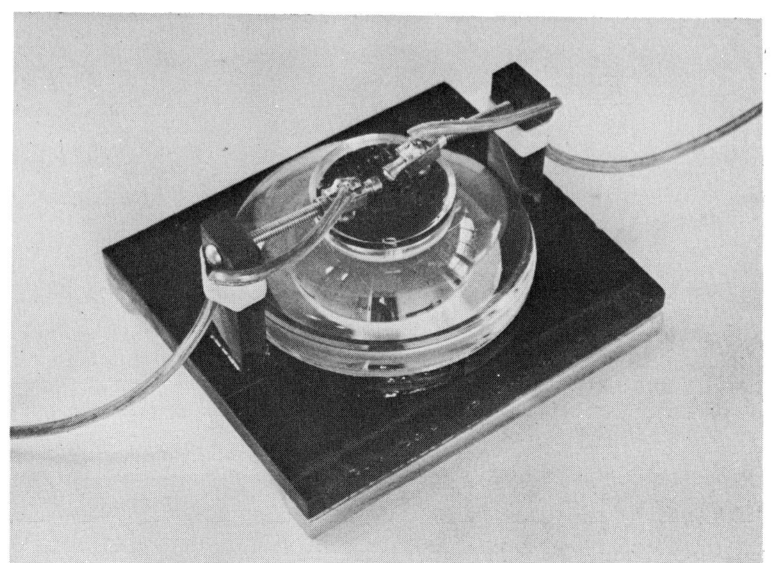

Fig. 8.24 Completed light collecting system with CdS photocell. It is supported on a "Perspex" stirrup that fits over a metal plate below the masking board.

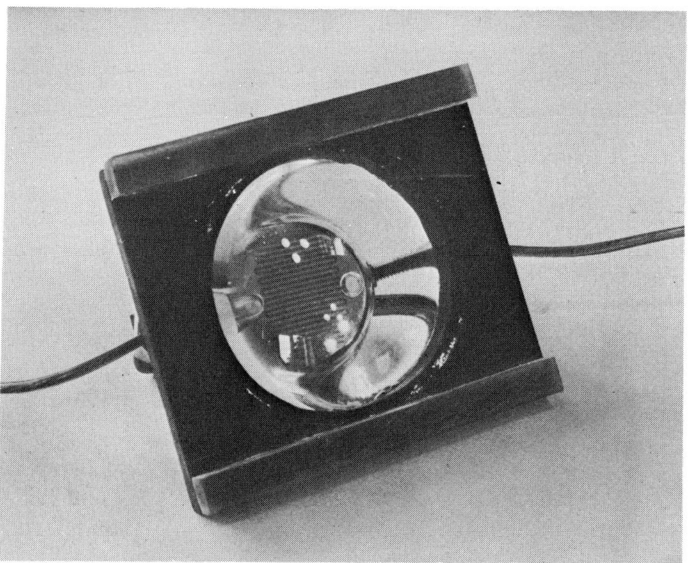

Fig. 8.25 Underside of light-collecting photocell unit showing the CdS cell through the lens.

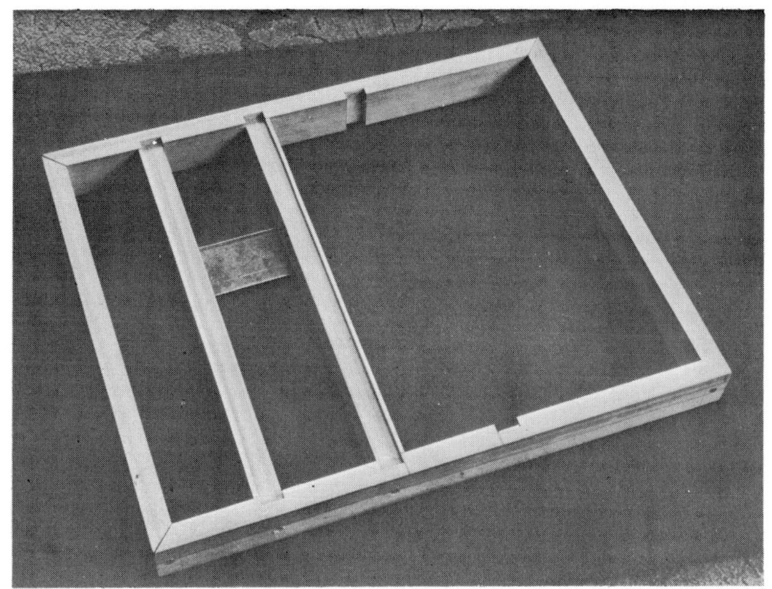

Fig. 8.26 Wooden frame for the masking board. The two cross members carry a metal plate to support the photocell assembly.

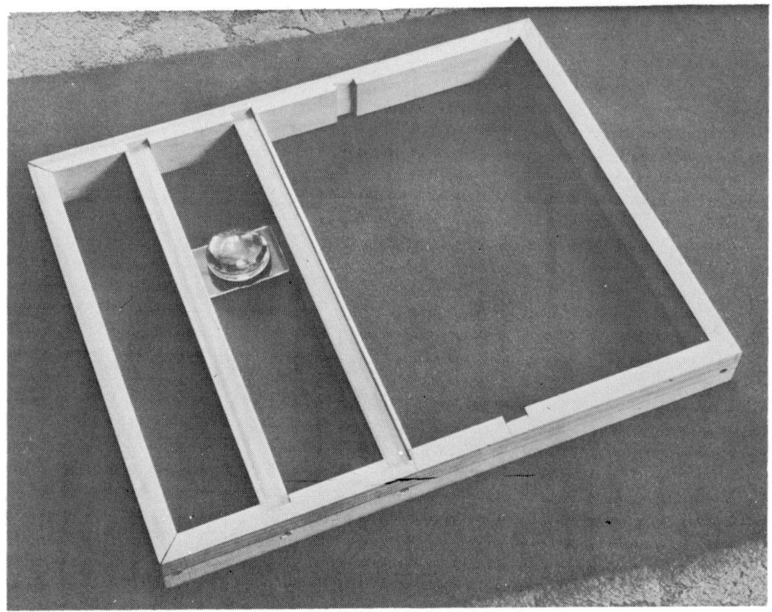

Fig. 8.27 Masking board frame with mirror and lens in position.

It was intended originally to position the photocell and lens in the geometric centre of the working surface but second thoughts revealed this to be undesirable as far more small prints are made than large, and a central position would involve unnecessary adjustments of the masking blades. A position was chosen that places the aperture in a corner of a half-plate enlargement and this is equally suitable for larger prints. It might be helpful to have the cell centrally placed for making a long run of big prints and it would be a simple matter to provide this alternative. I have already cut the recesses to take an additional crosswise batten and these can be seen in the illustrations.

The metal plate between the cross battens is of thin brass and two of its edges are turned up at right-angles by about $\frac{1}{16}$ in. so that a $2\frac{1}{2}$ x $3\frac{1}{2}$ in. handbag mirror sits snugly in the depression so provided. There is no need to cement the mirror in place and it can be cleaned or replaced easily whenever necessary.

A simple stirrup of wood or Perspex with a circular aperture to take the ring for supporting the bi-convex lens is built to suit the size of mirror used. I have used Perspex as it is an excellent material for accurate fabrication. The cement used for sticking Perspex hardens rapidly and enables construction to continue without delays. The ring support for the lens has been cemented in the aperture in the stirrup so that the lower pole of the lens almost touches the surface of the mirror. The "Perspex" uprights cemented close to the lens-supporting ring and diametrically opposed, hold the CdS cell face down and almost touching the upper pole of the lens. The author's cell has two short stiff wire connectors protruding from the back and it was easy to contrive a supporting and connection system with the aid of binding posts removed from a derelict three-pin, 5-amp plug. The support and connections must be designed so that they obstruct as little light as possible.

The whole photocell assembly is complete in itself and can be placed in position from underneath the paper-holder and removed when necessary. This is important as, when once the plywood and tinplate have been fixed to the top of the frame, access to underneath will not be easy. If desired,

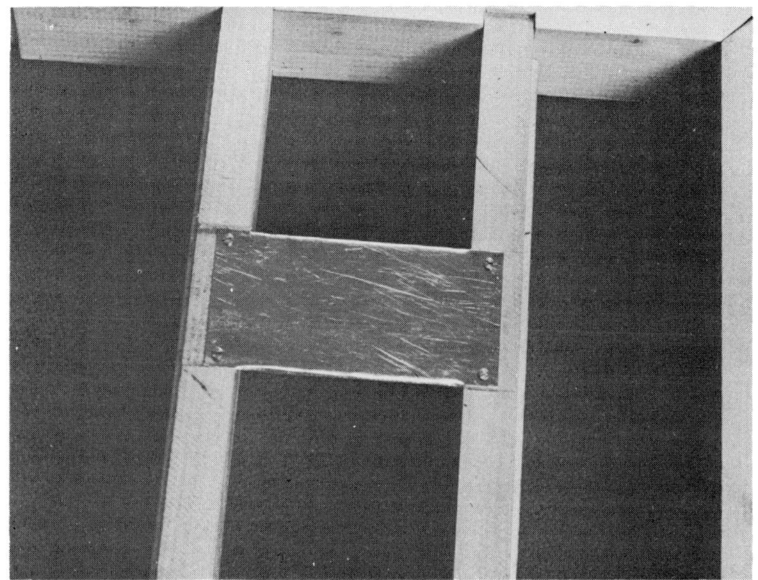

Fig. 8.28 *Underside of masking board frame showing metal plate screwed to cross members.*

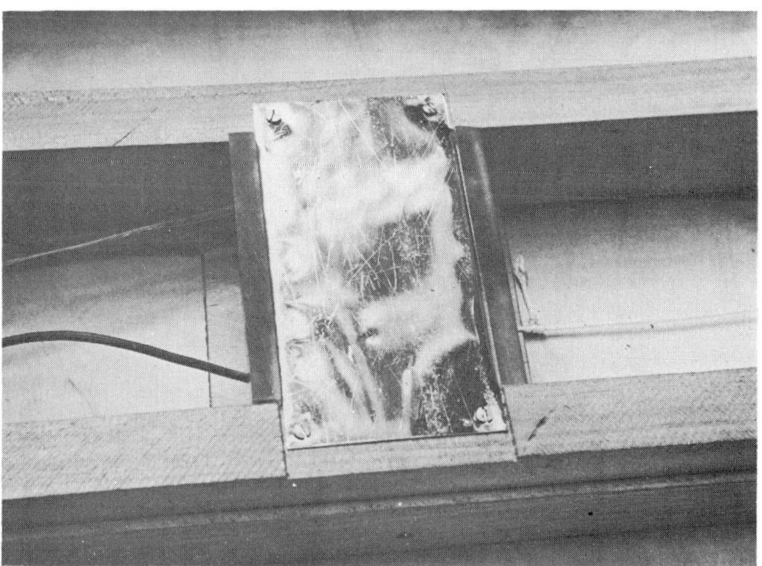

Fig. 8.29 *Metal plate with "Perspex" stirrup in position. The wires from the CdS cell can be seen and the nylon cord operating the sliding neutral density filter.*

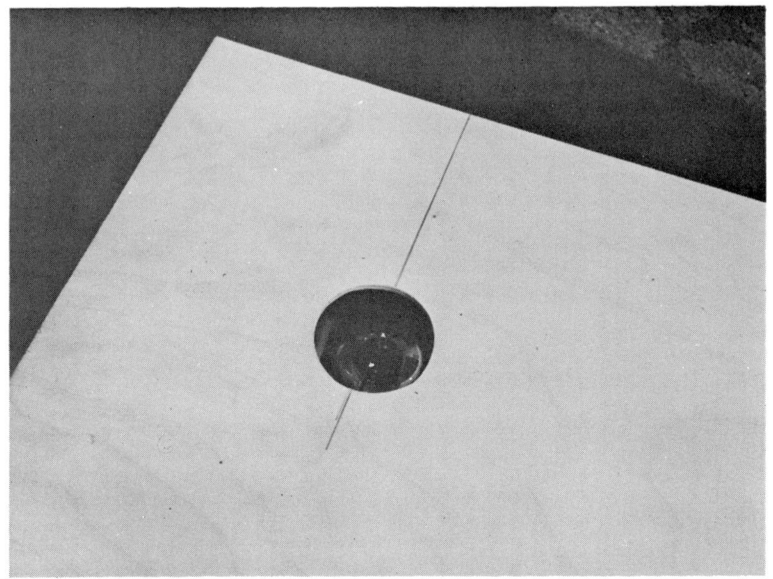

Fig. 8.30 Circular aperture in masking board showing photocell unit below.

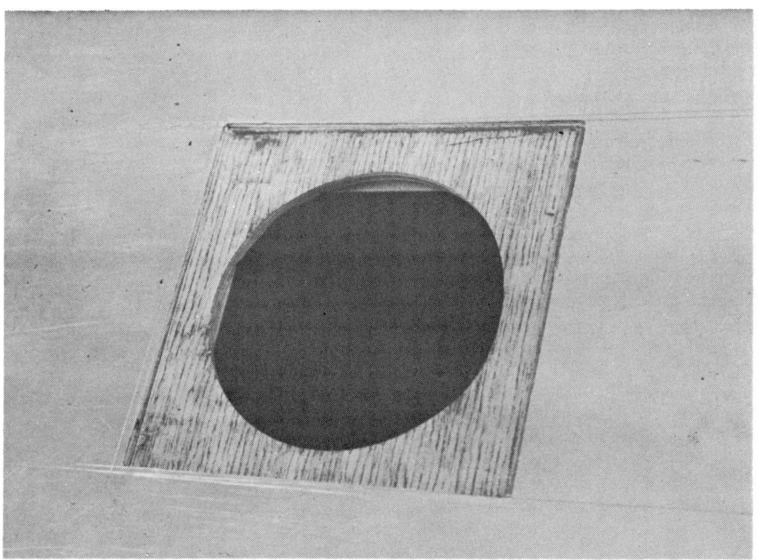

Fig. 8.31 Recess in plywood to take lantern slide cover glass that serves to protect photocell assembly from dust.

small turnbuttons of wood or plastic can be fixed to hold the photocell assembly in place firmly so that there is no worry should the holder be turned bodily on end. For the same reason it may be as well to secure the lens to its supporting ring with cement or adhesive tape. The latter will keep out the dust and eliminate the need for constant cleaning.

It was decided that, on balance, the most satisfactory method of securing the required x10 range shift was to use a neutral density filter of 1.0 immediately above the lens and photocell. It is for this reason that the two cross battens are specified as being narrower than the frame itself. It can be seen from the photographs that these are slightly lower than the top of the frame and this provides the space necessary to accommodate a neutral density filter 3 in. square, in a plywood holder. A strip of plywood has been screwed to the top outside edge of each cross batten and these strips form a track in which the filter can slide. The filter is of gelatine film and is 3 in. square and it has to be supported in a double frame of 1 mm plywood with an aperture $2\frac{3}{4}$ in. square in the geometric centre. The gelatine is sandwiched between the two thicknesses of plywood. Modern gelatine filters are lacquered and are reasonably damp-resistant. They can also be dusted with a soft brush without risk of scratches.

The filter in its holder is held in front of the photocell by means of two lengths of elastic, one attached to each side of the plywood frame. Stops are provided on the track to prevent the frame being pulled too far. A length of thin nylon cord attached to the opposite side of the filter frame and emerging from the front of the paper-holder, enables the filter to be pulled right out of the light path. Two further wooden stops glued in the track serve to indicate when the filter is out of operation. The plywood top of the paper holder prevents the filter holder riding up out of its track.

The whole thickness of the photocell assembly has been kept to about $1\frac{3}{4}$ in. and this means that it is wholly within the depth of the paper-holder even with the neutral density filter track taking up nearly $\frac{1}{4}$ in. Should circumstances make the unit deeper than this it may be necessary to lower it in the

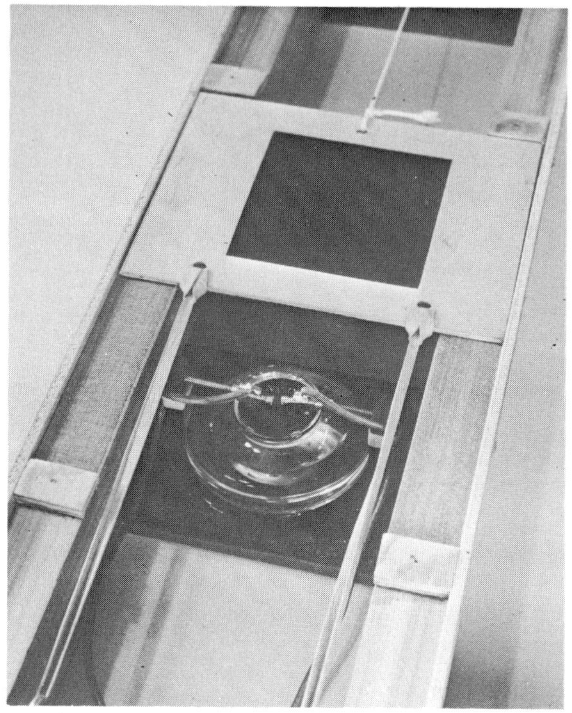

Fig. 8.32 Neutral density filter in thin plywood frame pulled clear of photocell assembly. The filter has a density of 1.0 to give a range shift of 10 to 1.

frame so that it does not foul the sliding filter. The metal plate can be lowered by putting washers under the screws that hold it to the battens but the frame will have now to be provided with rubber feet so that the plate and its screws do not cause the holder to rock on the enlarger baseboard.

When such adjustments have been attended to, the plywood top can be screwed in place after the necessary circular aperture has been cut in it. The tinplate could be screwed on also, but it is preferable to stick it on with an impact adhesive so that it is as flat as possible. The metal must be cleaned free of all grease to ensure a good bond. Just in case the whole thing has to be taken apart at any time the tinplate can be drilled with holes corresponding to the heads of the screws securing the plywood.

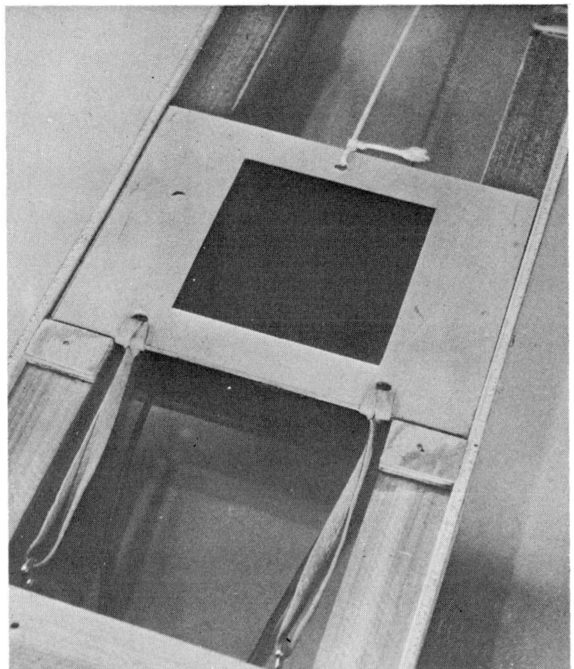

Fig. 8.33 Neutral density filter in place over photocell unit.

Some details of the construction of the paper-holder are shown in the photographs reproduced on pages 121 and 122. The mechanical arrangements for the sliding neutral density filter are illustrated in photographs on pages 118 and 119. The filter itself is sandwiched between two rectangles of very thin plywood which are cemented together with tube glue. A paper mask, which cannot be seen, has been included in the sandwhich so that the gelatine filter is not held by the glue. Being free at the edges the filter does not cockle unduly with changes in temperature and humidity. This is unimportant optically but a bulging filter may foul the photocell assembly immediately below it.

The stops that limit the travel of the filter in both directions are of $\frac{1}{8}$ in. plywood glued and pinned to the upper edges of the two cross battens. Three $\frac{3}{16}$ in. holes are drilled in the plywood filter-holder in the positions

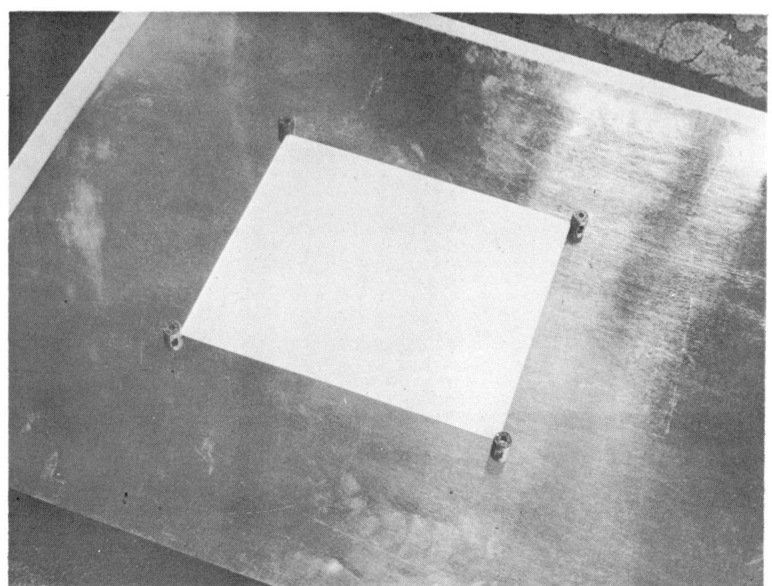

Fig. 8.34 Masking board covered with thin tinplate showing the use of small button magnets to hold the printing paper in position.

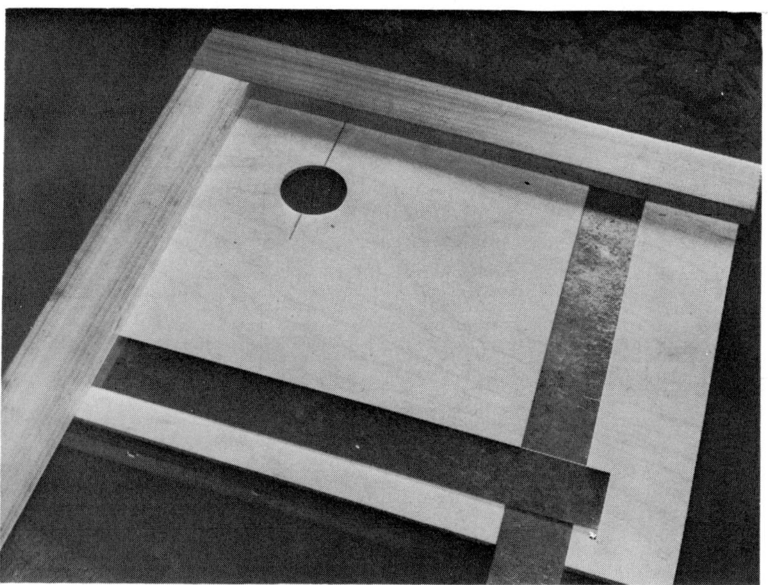

Fig. 8. 35 Wooden side members and metal mask blades roughly assembled to show basic construction.

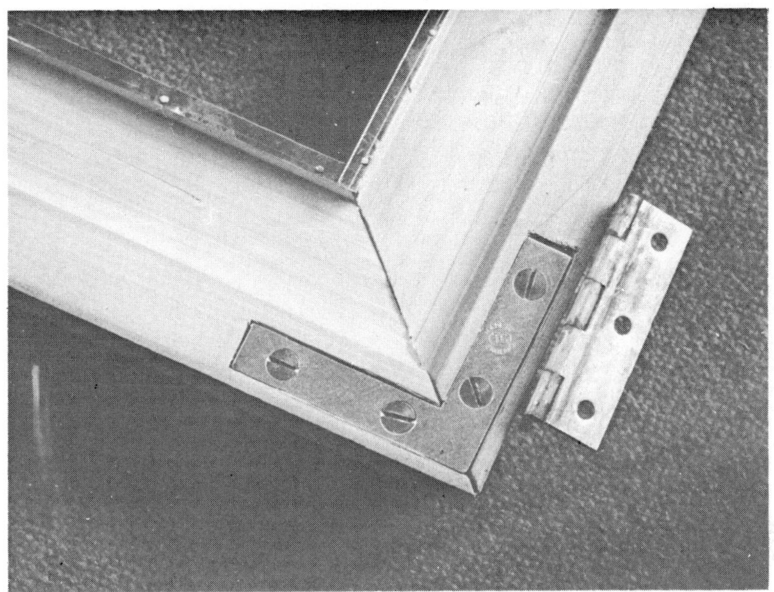

Fig. 8.36 Underside of wooden members showing channel to accommodate paper stop strips. The metal reinforcing plate is sunk flush.

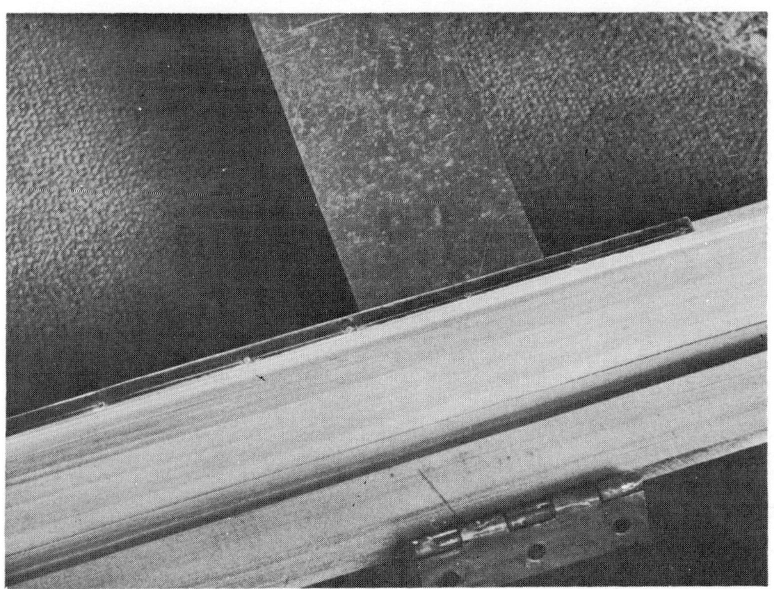

Fig. 8.37 Narrow metal strips pinned to underside of wooden members to form clean mask edge.

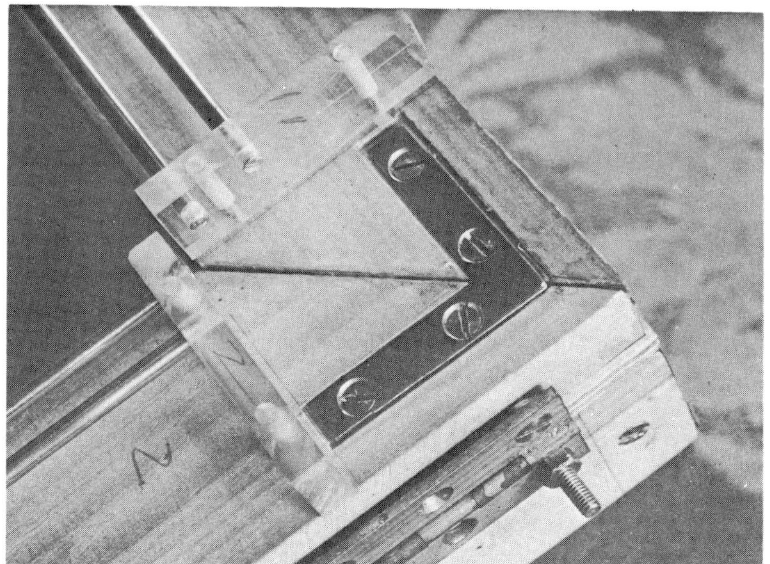

Fig. 8.38 Corner of masking frame showing "Perspex" blocks that support the stainless steel rods. One of the brass hinges can be seen.

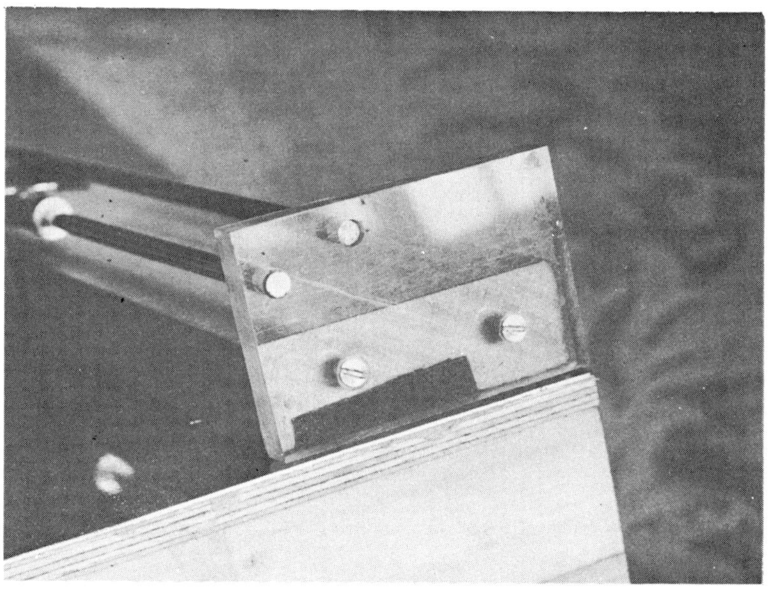

Fig. 8.39 "Perspex" plate on end of wooden member and supporting the outer ends of the steel rods.

shown. Two of these holes are to take the rubber bands which keep the filter in the light path at all times unless it is deliberately pulled out. The third hole takes the end of a length of thin nylon cord, the other end of which passes through a small hole drilled in the front of the paper-holder and terminates in a suitable handle for location in the dark. The free loops of the rubber bands are secured by means of two small screw hooks in the rear of the frame.

The functioning of the filter should be checked to make sure that, when the pull cord is released, it is returned fully into the light path. This can be done properly only when the plywood top has been screwed to the frame.

Figures 8.24 and 8.25 show the photocell assembly in its final form. The stirrup construction that enables the unit to sit snugly over the metal plate carrying the mirror is evident from the illustration. It has been found that there is just room to insert and remove the assembly from underneath the paper-holder, but while doing this the N.D. filter should be pulled out of the way to prevent its being scratched. A two-pin socket let into the rear of the frame takes the two connections to the photocell. Plenty of free wire should be allowed in making the connections between cell and socket so that there is no need to break soldered joints when the cell unit has to be removed for any reason. Surplus wire should be clipped securely out of the way so that it cannot interfere with the filter mechanism or wander into the optical system. Figures 8.32 and 8.33 are of the rear of the paper holder and shows the mirror plate, photocell assembly and N.D. filter in their correct positions.

It may not be quite clear from a reproduced photograph how the photocell is supported above the bi-convex lens and provided with connecting wires. Two "Perspex" uprights are cemented to the baseplate of the stirrup and abutting the ring that supports the lens. These pillars are drilled at the top to take the B.A. screws, the latter terminating in binding posts from an old three-pin plug. The stiff wires protruding from the back of the CdS cell are clamped by the binding posts and so also are the bared ends of the connecting wires. To make sure of permanent low-resistance connections at these points the clamped wires are also soldered. Excessive

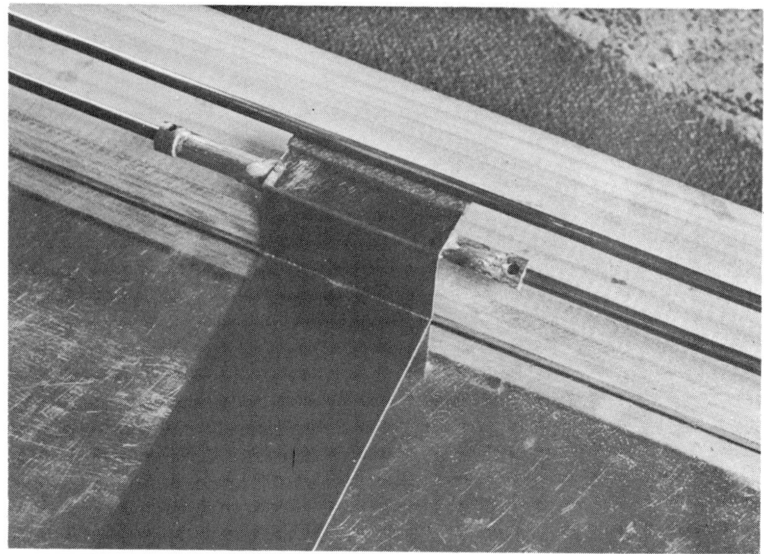

Fig. 8.40 Method of supporting metal mask strips on stainless steel rods using brass tube. "Meccano" collars have been soldered to the ends of the tube, their centre holes having been reamed out to 3/16 in. diameter.

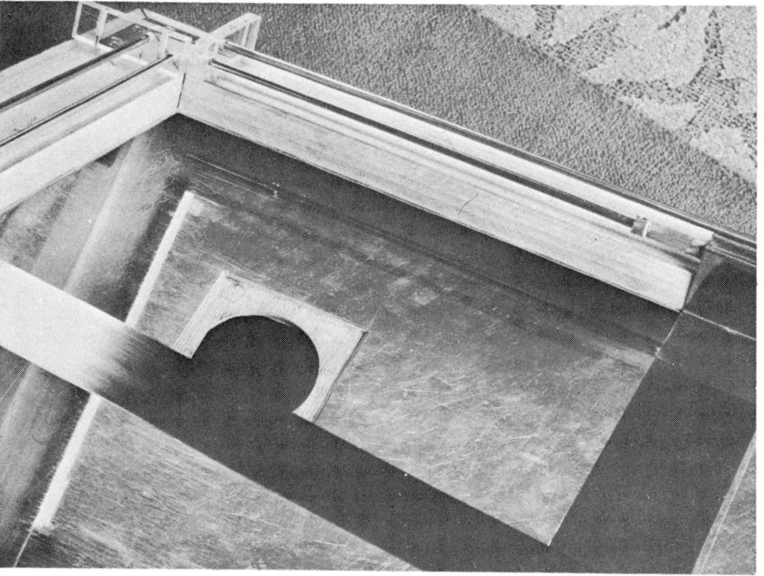

Fig. 8.41 Masking frame lifted to show paper stop strips beneath.

heat should be avoided for fear of softening the plastic encapsulation of the cell.

Figure 8.31 is of the circular aperture in the plywood surface through which light from the enlarger lens reaches the photocell. Around the aperture is cut a recess about $\frac{1}{32}$ in. deep and $3\frac{1}{4}$ in. square to take a dust cover in the form of a lantern slide cover glass. The recess is made by cutting away two layers of the plywood — very easy to do with a sharp knife and a chisel. A similar square aperture has to be cut in the sheet of tinplate that covers the plywood as previously described. This involves drilling a row of closely spaced holes just within the outline of the square, joining up the holes with a small file and removing the cut-out portion. The ragged edges of the aperture are quickly smoothed with a medium-cut file.

To cement the tinplate to the plywood, Evo-stik Resin W has been found very effective. The metal should be cleaned to remove all traces of grease and any small buckles resulting from cutting and drilling should be flattened with a hammer. The resin adhesive should be applied freely to the surface of the wood only, spreading it to an even film with the edge of a piece of card. The tinplate is now lowered into position and pressed firmly into contact. Unlike a contact adhesive, the resin allows the tinplate to be moved into place should it have been wrongly positioned in the first instance. Light, even pressure over the whole surface of the metal and maintained overnight ensures a good bond and a level surface. Any resin oozing at the edges can be trimmed away with a knife. It is assumed that the metal has been drilled at the edges to correspond with the screws securing the plywood to the wooden frame. This is desirable in case it becomes necessary to remove the plywood for any reason.

It is as well to defer covering the tinplate with matt white material until all the constructional work has been completed as the fabric is easily soiled. When it is done, a small overlap of the adhesive material over the edges of the lantern slide cover glass covering the photocell aperture will hold it securely and keep dust out of the optical system.

The masking frame of the paper-holder can be added or it can be dispensed with if white borders are not required. In this event, the printing paper is held flat with four small button magnets just nipping the corners of the sheet. There is no difficulty in positioning the paper relative to the image on the easel. A sheet of stout white paper the same size as the printing paper to be used is employed for focusing and composing the image. If the magnets are placed along two adjacent edges of the paper used for focusing to mark its position, the printing paper can be substituted for it with absolute accuracy. The magnets are then transferred to the extreme corners of the paper to hold it flat.

The wooden part of the masking frame is made by joining two lengths of $2\frac{1}{2}$ x $\frac{7}{8}$ in. hardwood together at right-angles using a mitred joint reinforced by means of right-angled brass or steel repair plates let into the wood. It is important that the right-angle joint should be exactly 90° otherwise print masking will be out of square. The under-sides of the wooden battens have to be channelled with a plough before assembly to a depth of $\frac{1}{4}$ in. and a width of $1\frac{1}{2}$ in. at a distance of $\frac{1}{8}$ in. from the inside edge. The purpose of the channel is

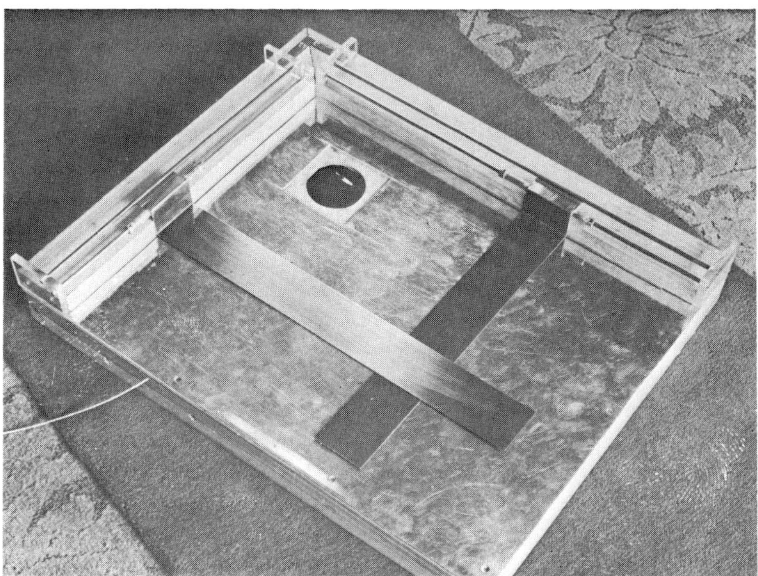

Fig. 8.42 Masking board complete except for covering of tinplate with white adhesive material and painting the mask matt black.

to accommodate the paper stop strips controlling the width of the print border which can be made adjustable from ¼ in. to about 1 in.

The adjustable mask blades are 2 in. wide and are cut from a chromium-plated glazing sheet that has outlived its usefulness for its intended purpose through an accumulation of scratches. It is helpful if the metal strips can be cut on a guillotine designed for sheet metal as it avoids the distortion resulting from the use of tin snips. The strips have two right-angle bends in them as can be seen from the photographs on page 124. The strips slide along a pair of $\frac{1}{16}$ in. diameter stainless steel rods mounted in blocks of $\frac{5}{16}$ in. "Perspex" screwed to the wooden members of the mask frame. Small 2 BA setscrews hold the rods securely in their holes in the "Perspex" blocks (Figure 8.43). The second of the two rods prevents

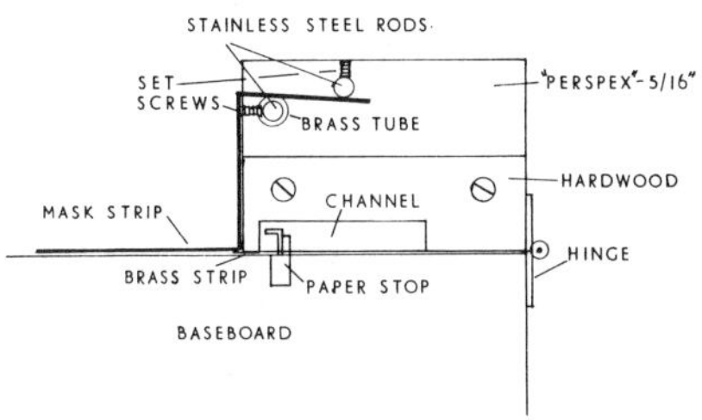

Fig. 8.43 Sectional view showing the method of mounting the masking blades using stainless steel rods and metal tubes.

the masking blade from falling down as the frame is lifted to place a sheet of printing paper in position. Short lengths of $\frac{3}{16}$ in. internal diameter brass tube attached to the mask strips allow the latter to slide along the rods. It is advisable to cement the tubes to the strips using "Araldite" adjusting the strips so that they give a perfect right-angled mask corner and then allowing the adhesive to cure overnight.

If it is impossible to find brass tube that is a nice sliding fit on the stainless steel rods, larger diameter tubes can be used at the ends of which have been soldered "Meccano" collars (Part No. 59), their holes being reamed out from their $\frac{5}{32}$ in. diameter to a good fit on the rods.

The paper stops controlling the position of the paper underneath the mask frame are made from right-angled pieces cut from lengths of brass, "H"-section curtain rail. An 11 in. and a 13 in. length are suitable for paper sizes up to 12 x 15 in. Brass pegs, $\frac{3}{16}$ in. in diameter and about $\frac{1}{4}$ in. long are soldered to the paper stop bars and suitable holes are drilled in the masking board to position the stop bars for different widths of white border. This calls for careful drilling but it is not unduly difficult. Narrow strips of thin brass are pinned along the inside edges of the wooden mask members so that they protrude about $\frac{1}{8}$ in. beyond the wood to give clean-cut mask edges.

The mask frame is hinged to the baseboard and it is convenient to use 2 BA screws and wing nuts to secure the hinges to the baseboard so that the whole frame can be removed in a moment should it be wished to discard it for making big prints without white borders. The masking frame itself should be spray-painted matt black using one of the "Aerosol" sprays on the market.

CHAPTER NINE

SPEEDS OF PRINTING PAPERS

It is not usual for manufacturers to quote speeds for their printing papers except in very general relative turns. Ilford, for example, state that the speeds of their Ilfobrom papers are the same for all grades based on the exposure required to produce a mid-tone density of 0.7, with the exception of the hardest grade of all, No. 5, which is approximately half the speed of the other grades. The current Kodak bromide papers are similarly the same speed except for the hardest grade which is again half the speed of the others. The speed criterion for Kodak papers is that specified in American Standard Ph 2 : 2—1966 which is the exposure required to yield a density of 0.6. The same Standard defines American Standard paper speed as being equal to $10^3/E_{0.6}$ where $E_{0.6}$ is the exposure required in metre-candle seconds to yield a density of 0.6 with a specified degree of development.

It has been found that Ilford and Kodak bromide papers have the same speeds in practice which is very convenient. A little thought will show that the criterion on which the speed of a paper is based should depend on the method used for estimating printing exposures. If a trial and error method is employed a speed number based on the exposure required to produce a medium density is appropriate because the depth of a print is normally judged on the basis of a middle tone. In this respect the small density difference between the Ilford and Kodak speed criteria is unimportant.

When using an enlarging photometer the speed criterion must be appropriate to the method of use of the meter. If spot measurements are made of the darkest tone in the image in which detail can be seen, then paper speeds based on the exposure required to produce a very low density are required as the darkest tone in the image on the enlarger baseboard is a subject highlight. It is difficult to specify precisely the low value of density on which highlight speeds should be based but a value of 0.04 is just readily discernible from the white of the paper alone and it is the density at which the lower limiting point on the paper curve is located according to American Standard Ph 2 : 2—1966.

At the other end of the scale, if a photometer is used for making spot measurements of the lightest part of the image in which detail can be seen, paper speeds should be based on the exposure that produces a density just distinguishable from the maximum black of the paper. Again it might be reasonable to base the speed on a density equal to $0.9\,D_{m'ax}$ which is the density corresponding to the upper limiting point on the paper curve according to American Standard Ph 2 : 2—1966.

When using an enlarging exposure meter for integrated measurements of the light on the enlarger easel or, what amounts to the same thing, when basing printing exposures on the $\bar{D}$ of negatives, none of the foregoing paper speed criteria is ideal. The author has carried out a great deal of work in this field and, as mentioned in Chapter Six, a paper speed based on the exposure required to yield a density of 1.10 above base plus fog density for glossy papers and a density of 0.75 for matt papers is proposed. The revision of American Standard Ph 2 : 2 in 1966 has caused this proposal to be altered a little because of a completely different method of evaluating the log exposure range of papers which gives generally smaller values than the method specified in the 1953 version of the Standard. (Figure 9.1)

The modified proposal is for speed numbers based on a density of 1.0 above base and fog density for glossy papers and 0.70 for matt papers. For semi-matt papers a density of 0.85 above base and fog has been found suitable. In practical work, these densities are not critical but it is important that speed numbers based on a middle density shall be employed with an integrating photometry system rather than speeds based on a very high or very low density. It has been found that when using Ilford and Kodak papers, an integrating photometer gives tolerably good results if all grades but the very hardest of all are treated as having identical speeds. Small errors may be encountered because of minor batch-to-batch speed variations which are unavoidable in the manufacture of sensitive materials.

American Standard Ph 2 : 2—1966 includes in an appendix a formula for working out exposure times in printing based on the ASA speed —

$$ t = \frac{k}{I_{av} \times S} $$

where k is a constant of about 1,000 when I_{av} is in metre-candles, I_{av} is the average illumination in the exposure plane, and S is the ASA paper speed. This formula is appropriate when enlarging exposures are estimated on the basis of integrated measurement of the light falling on the baseboard or, what amounts to the same thing, on the total density of negatives.

The author has found it difficult to reconcile the use of a paper speed based on the exposure required to produce a density of 0.6 above base plus fog in this formula with the results of his own work in this field. There is a simple method of arriving at the density on which paper should be based using an enlarger photometer/timer such as the "Revomatic" described on page 75. If this is set up so that it gives prints of satisfactory density from negatives of balanced density distribution the following procedure can be employed.

A standard negative is enlarged and a sheet of paper exposed by means of the photometer/timer. The "Revomatic" measures the light reflected from the surface of the paper while it is being exposed and switches the enlarger lamp off at the end of the exposure time. The negative is removed from the carrier and a second sheet of paper is exposed without the negative and the photometer, reading the much brighter light from the paper gives a shorter exposure time. The two sheets of paper are processed together and the result is a good print and a sheet of paper fogged evenly all over. The density of the fog is the density on which paper speed should be based for this method of exposure estimation. For glossy papers this fog has measured from 1.0 to 1.1 time and time again. Even with semi-matt papers

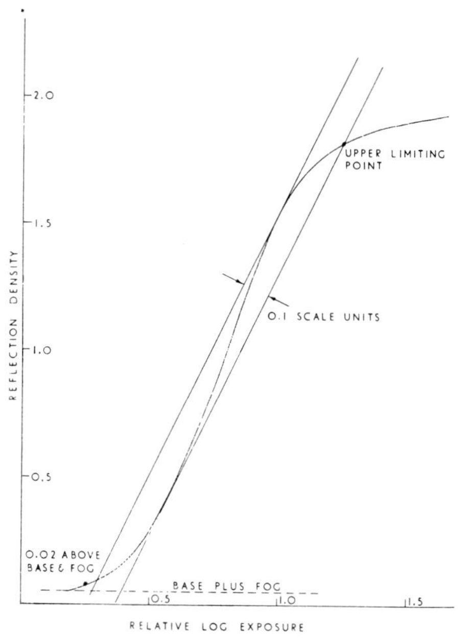

Fig. 9.1 Characteristic curve of a printing paper showing the location of the upper and lower limiting points in accordance with American Standard Ph2:2–1953. The revised version of the Standard dated 1966 specifies a different method for locating these two points.

the density obtained by this experimental procedure has never been as low as 0.6.

Lengthy correspondence with those in U.S.A. concerned with the researches leading to this standard finally produced the following admission —

"You do indeed have good evidence that, for an optimum print, a reflection density of about 1.1 above fog-plus-base density corresponds to the total transmittance of the negative. One reason for our, apparently-incorrect, estimate of 0.6 instead of 1.1 is that our first-choice prints seem to be lighter than yours and perhaps too light."

The individual is normally compelled to determine the speeds of the papers he uses, selecting a criterion to suit the measurement system he employs. This may be done by ordinary trial and error methods as each grade of paper is used. This takes a little time but when once it has been done it does not have to be repeated. When a batch of paper has to be changed for another a quick test is all that is required to discover any small speed difference between the two batches. Such differences are much smaller than they used to be as manufacturers find more effective methods of ensuring batch-to-batch uniformity.

A speedier and more elegant method of determining paper speeds on any basis involves the use of a step-wedge. This can be built up from strips of gelatine neutral density filters or obtained from makers such as Ilford or Kodak Ltd. Both undertake to make wedges to meet individual requirements but one-off wedges are naturally expensive. The important requirement is that a wedge for paper speed evaluation should have a nominal density increment of 0.10. This enables speeds to be determined to within $1°$ on a log scale or to $\frac{1}{2}°$ by interpolation. It is possible to obtain inexpensive wedges with a nominal increment of 0.15 which enables speed to be evaluated to within $1\frac{1}{2}°$, or less by interpolation.

Up to a few years ago, Kodak Ltd. offered a wide range of "density strips" or step-wedges on film and this included at least one with a nominal increment of 0.10. The range was reduced to three in number and the only density increments available are 0.15 and 0.30. The former is adequate although not ideal and the Kodak photographic step-tablet No. 2 is obtainable through a dealer at a price of under a pound at the time of writing. It has an effective area of $\frac{7}{8}$ x $4\frac{1}{8}$ inches with 21 steps and a range of about 3.0. This range means that a sample exposed behind the wedge receives a range of exposures of about 1,000 to 1.

A step-wedge with a nominal density increment of 0.10 is obtainable from the publishers of this book, Fountain Press,

46/47 Chancery Lane, London WC2A 1JU at a price of £2 post free. This is only a fraction of the cost of a similar wedge made to individual specifications and is made possible by having a large batch manufactured.

A wedge for paper speed testing should be mounted on clean glass of a size to fit an available printing frame and all clear glass surrounding the wedge must be masked off with black paper. In the absence of a printing frame, the wedge can be mounted on glass about $\frac{1}{8}$ in. thick which is heavy enough to hold the wedge in contact with the paper samples on the enlarger baseboard. The steps of the wedge have to be numbered for easy identification and, so that the numbers of the steps can be read off directly as paper speed indices, the scale of numbers should be from 1 to 30 the numbers increasing with density. The numbers can be put on a sheet of clear film using "Letraset" or "Driprint" using figures of a suitable size for the width of the wedge steps and the film laid over the wedge to serve as protection for it. The numbers should be on the under-side of the cover film to protect them from abrasion and this will mean that the figures are right-reading on all exposed and processed samples. When the cover film becomes soiled through use it can be renewed and at all times the wedge itself is kept clean.

To find the relative speeds of a number of papers a sample of each is exposed behind the wedge for a time long enough for accurate control. The minimum time should be regarded as being 5 seconds and it is vital that all the samples being tested shall have identical exposures otherwise the speed numbers arrived at will be in error. Ideally, the lamp used as an exposing source should be connected to a controlled voltage supply but this is not strictly necessary unless it is known that the mains supply is subject to short-term voltage variations.

The light from the enlarger lens is a suitable exposing source and by altering the height of the enlarger and the lens aperture the illumination on the wedge can be controlled to bring the exposure time to a suitable level. This is such that all exposed and processed samples show a full black and a pure white. This is not difficult to achieve as the wedge gives a range of exposures of 1,000 to 1 whereas the softest grade of paper requires a range of exposures of no more than about 50 to 1 to produce both a black and a white. There is thus considerable exposure latitude.

All the exposed samples should be developed together in fresh developer of the kind normally used, for 2 minutes at 68° F. This is a degree of development at about the middle of the development amplitude of most papers giving room for manoeuvre both ways in actual printing. Agitation should be vigorous and continuous as is customary in the development of papers. At the end of the development time the strips are transferred together to an acid stop bath and moved around quickly to stop development at once. After about 10 seconds in the stop bath they are transferred to fresh acid fixer for 5 minutes, washed briefly, and then blotted.

There is no need to dry the samples before assigning speeds to the papers but they are easier to handle if allowed to dry. The normal grade of paper will have to be assigned an arbitrary speed number but before this can be done it has to be decided what criterion will be used. It is quite simple to assign highlight, shadow and mid-tone speeds to all the papers and, at this point, reference must be made to the six wedge strips reproduced on page 136. These are of six grades of glossy papers all exposed and processed identically and the grade numbers 0 to 5 and indicated in the illustration. The highlight tones having a density nearest to 0.04 are marked with a black dot and it is on these steps that highlight speed numbers will be based. The tone just removed from full black on each strip is indicated also — the white dots at the top, and a mid-tone with a density as close as possible to 1.0 above base and fog density is marked as well with a white dot.

It will be noticed that, in some cases, the dots, both black and white are between two steps. This is the result of interpolation where this was necessary. As far as shadow and highlight speeds are concerned, the numbers of the marked steps can be taken as the speed indices. Thus the normal grade has a highlight speed of 19° and a shadow speed of 9½° the white dot in this case falling between steps 9 and 10. Similarly, speed indices for integrating photometry can be taken as the numbers of the marked mid-tone steps but a word of caution is necessary here. In using an integrating photometer on the enlarger easel, a diffuser is placed in front of the enlarger lens. This introduces some loss of light by scattering and hence the effective mid-tone speeds of the papers relative to their highlight and shadow speeds will be

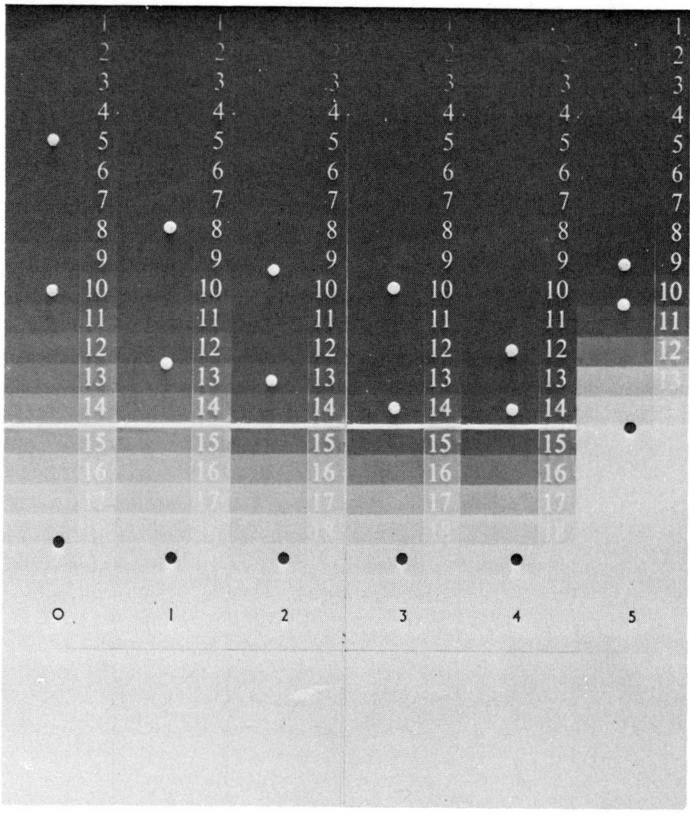

Fig. 9.2 Wedge exposures of six grades of glossy bromide papers showing the speeds of the papers on three different bases — shadow, highlight and mid-tone. The logarithmic speed numbers for these papers are shown in the table on page 137.

higher by a degree or two than those evaluated from the wedge tests.

The important thing to remember here is that any one set of speeds — highlight, shadow or mid-tone will be relatively correct no matter what. For example, the normal grade of paper (2) has a mid-tone speed which is 3° higher than the mid-tone speed of grade 0 which means it is twice as fast. Grades 1, 2, 3 and 4 all have equal highlight speeds and so forth.

For six such grades of paper we can arrive at 18 speed indices and these should all be set down in tabular form as shown below. Having done this, the general level of all the

PAPER SPEEDS

The logarithmic speed numbers (relative) in the table below are derived from the wedge tests reproduced on page 136.

Paper Grade	Speed Numbers		
	Shadow	Mid-tone	Highlight
0	$5°$	$10°$	$18\frac{1}{2}°$
1	$8°$	$12\frac{1}{2}°$	$19°$
2	$9\frac{1}{2}°$	$13°$	$19°$
3	$10°$	$14°$	$19°$
4	$12°$	$14°$	$19°$
5	$9°$	$10\frac{1}{2}°$	$14\frac{1}{2}°$

numbers can be raised or lowered as desired by adding or subtracting the same number for each index. This may be desirable to fit in with any calculation system that may be devised by the individual. From the tests reproduced on page 136 it is evident that we cannot subtract a number larger than 5 from the speeds as this would make the shadow speed of grade 0 a minus number which could cause confusion and error. There is no limit to the magnitude of the number that could be added to all the speeds; they could be pushed into the hundreds if, for any reason, this size of number were wanted.

An interesting side-issue emerges from the shadow and highlight speed numbers found in this way. If the latter is subtracted from the former and the answer divided by 10, the result is the approximate log exposure range of the paper is question. For example, taking grade 2 with shadow and highlight speed indices of $9\frac{1}{2}$ and 19 respectively, the difference between these is $9\frac{1}{2}$ or 9.5. Dividing this figure by

10 the answer is 0.95 which is the approximate log exposure range of this particular normal grade. Values for log exposures range obtained in this way are not likely to agree with those obtained by more rigorous sensitometric methods but they are likely to agree with measurements on the enlarger easel with a spot photometer designed to indicate the most suitable grade of paper for the negative being enlarged. The instructions accompanying most spot photometers include directions for this operation. The author is doubtful of the usefulness of the method except perhaps for the absolute beginner.

The low intensity reciprocity failure of printing papers is of sufficient magnitude for it to matter in enlarging photometry. It is rarely discussed specifically in textbooks but at least one enlarging exposure calculator on the market includes correction for reciprocity failure in its circuitry.

Unfortunately, the extent of low-intensity reciprocity failure varies from one make of paper to another and even among different grades of the same paper. To quote a specific example, a print that required 10 seconds exposure at a particular degree of enlargement, and calculated to require 50 seconds exposure at a larger magnification, in fact had to be given 80 seconds to achieve an adequately dark print. The calculation of the exposure required at the larger magnification was on the basis of accurate measurement of the light intensity on the enlarger easel using a sensitive photo-electric photometer.

The spot photometers sold as enlarging exposure meters may include built-in correction for reciprocity failure but such corrections have to be for the average paper and cannot be correct for all papers. In practice, the phenomenon does not cause much difficulty as the tendency is to keep printing exposure times as constant as possible by making use of the lens apertures. This cannot be done in the case of big enlargements from dense negatives but even here, exposures of longer than say 60 seconds should be rare. In cases where exposure times are much longer than the usual 5 to 20 seconds it may be advisable to supplement the use of a photometer with a test exposure. With prolonged experience of a group of papers and a particular photometer it should be possible to arrive at the corrections that should be applied to unduly long estimated exposure times.

There is no need to use a step-wedge for determining paper speeds for use with an enlarging photometer. Most printers work with no more than three different grades except perhaps for very exceptional negatives and the speeds of three papers can be determined by making trial exposures. In setting up any system of photometry the first trial prints will fix the working speed of the normal grade and trial exposures from appropriate negatives on the other two grades will reveal their speeds. In the event of a full range of perhaps six grades being used regularly, it is worth setting aside a good negative that suits each of the grades. If these are always available, it is a simple matter to test any new paper or batch brought into use to ascertain its speed for the photometry system in use. Although wedge tests are quicker and more accurate if carried out with care, practical testing under normal working conditions is a wholly satisfactory method.

CHAPTER TEN

EXPOSURE RANGES OF PRINTING PAPERS

The subject of exposure range has been discussed briefly in earlier chapters but it calls for more detailed consideration as it is an important factor in the making of high-quality prints, more especially so if an enlarging photometer is being used.

It is probably true to say that there can never be a completely unequivocal method of specifying the upper and lower limiting points on the characteristic curve of a paper. That the matter is difficult is indicated by the many methods that have been proposed for doing it.

It has been proposed that the limiting points on a paper curve are those on the toe and shoulder at which the gradient is 0.2. It has been found however that, when a negative is flat and the paper therefore hard, a greater limiting gradient is required than when a negative is hard and the paper soft.

A further proposal was that the useful exposure limits of a paper are determined by points P and Q in Figure 10.1 where the gradient at P is a specified fraction — 0.2, or 0.1 — of the slope $\overline{G}$ of the line PQ which is tangential to the shoulder of the curve. P and Q mark the lower and upper limiting points on the curve and the interval between them measured on the log exposure axis is the logarithmic exposure range of paper.

This fractional gradient method of evaluating the exposure range of a paper was once recognised in American Standard Z38.2.3—1947 but it was replaced by a different method in the 1953 version of the same Standard in which it was stated that the revised method correlated very well with the fractional gradient method and had the advantage of easier application. Determination of fractional gradient points is difficult because of the need to satisfy two mutually dependent conditions at one and the same time. Because of these difficulties, accuracy was difficult to achieve in routine testing.

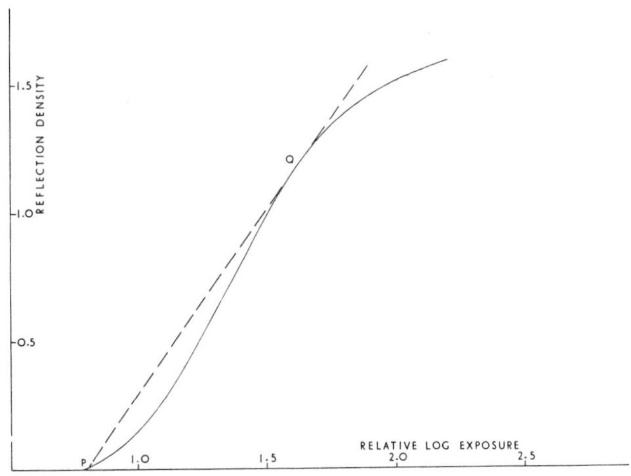

Fig. 10.1 One of the proposals for determining the useful exposure limits of a printing paper. This is a fractional gradient method and the gradient at point P is a specified fraction — 0.2 or 0.1 of the average gradient of the line PQ.

The method described in the 1953 American Standard is illustrated in Figure 9.1. The limiting point on the toe of the curve is located at a density of 0.02 above base plus fog density. The upper limiting point is located by means of a simple jig consisting of two parallel straight lines 0.1 scale units apart scribed on a sheet of clear film. The jig is positioned on the curve so that the left-hand line is tangential to the upper part of the curve and the right-hand line tangential to the bottom. Where the right-hand line cuts the shoulder of the curve is the upper limiting point. The exposure range of the paper is measured between these two points in terms of log exposure. The latter rounded off to the first decimal place was called the "scale index" of the paper and it was intended that manufacturers should state the scale indices of their papers for the guidance of users.

Although this Standard was not followed by a comparable British Standard, manufacturers have been following its provisions possibly in the interests of international standardisation. The 1966 version of the American Standard specifies yet another method for locating the two limiting points on a paper curve. These are illustrated in Figure 1.2. The lower limiting point is at a density of 0.04 above base and fog density. The upper limiting point is fixed at a density equal to $0.9D_{max}$ where D_{max} is the maximum density reached by the curve. The latter is considered to be a point on the shoulder of the curve where the gradient has fallen to 0.05 but it is sufficient to take the absolute maximum density shown by the curve. It is, in fact, difficult to measure such a low gradient accurately. The log exposure range of the paper is measured between the two limiting points along the log exposure axis of the curve.

This current Standard method of evaluating the log exposure range of a paper is considered to give a figure that agrees closely with the density range of the negatives most suitable for printing on it.

All the foregoing may appear to be a little theoretical and only remotely connected with the business of making high quality prints. It has an important practical significance in that, with a selective photometer used for on-easel evaluation, the brightness range of the enlarged image can be measured and a suitable grade of paper chosen. In this context it is essential to have a meaningful value for the log exposure range of a paper.

A suitable grade of paper can be chosen on the basis of the density range of a negative as measured with an ordinary transmission densitometer. This does not take into account the specularity of the enlarger or the effects of non-image forming light on the contrast of the image on the enlarger easel.

The best prints are not necessarily those made on a grade of paper chosen to match the density range of the negative. It is often essential to choose a harder grade of paper than is indicated by the density range of the negative and to resort to local exposure control to obtain the optimum result. This expedient is desirable with subjects showing large gaps in their tone scales as, for example, the room interior showing an exterior view through large windows. A straight print on a soft paper is likely to look unpleasantly flat but a dodged print on a harder grade will preserve the contrast of the interior and exterior detail the contrast compression being confined to the gap in the tone scale where it is often unnoticeable.

STOP PRESS

Just as this section on black and white printing reached the proof stage, particulars became available of the Philips Mini-timer (PDT 015). It comprises an enlarging focusing magnifier of the reflex type into which is built an integrated circuit which is connected to a CdS monocorn photocell. The latter is in a small housing on a support with a stand and it is positioned so that the cell collects the light from the printing paper on the enlarger easel as it is being exposed. When the enlarging exposure is started a button on the Mini-timer is depressed and a red pilot light glows. When the red light goes out the enlarger lamp is switched off to terminate the exposure.

The device has a dial numbered from 1 to 10 to cater for papers of various speeds and the exposure range covered by the dial is 10 to 1. The photometer is powered by a 9-volt PP3 battery which should last about a year. It indicates correct exposures for image sizes up to 12 x 16 in.

The Mini-timer is an integrating photometer and the numbered dial offers an opportunity for adjusting exposure levels to suit negatives having very large shadow areas or extensive highlights.

The quite diminutive electrical components are an indication of the probable compactness of future enlarging photometers.

CHAPTER ELEVEN

PRINCIPLES OF COLOUR PRINTING

Although the printing of a complementary colour negative on to a three-layer colour paper has much in common with black and white printing, there are certain differences that must be understood before any method of measurement can be used effectively.

A colour negative is three negatives in one. One is a record of the blue light reflected by the subject; the second is a record of the green light and the third image is a record of the red light. As these three negatives are firmly and irrevocably sandwiched together they would be indistinguishable one from the other if they were in the form of black metallic silver. They are therefore coloured; silver is replaced by dyes, yellow for the blue record, magenta for the green record, and cyan or blue-green for the red record. The yellow, magenta and cyan images control the amount of blue, green and red light reaching the paper imagewise so enabling a print to be made in which the yellow, magenta and cyan images are of the correct densities to produce a neutral balance — grey tones being reproduced without hue.

A silver image is usually neutral in colour and absorbs light of all wavelengths equally. Hence its density will be the same value no matter what the colour of the light used in the densitometer, and regardless of the spectral sensitivity of the light receiver — usually a photocell. The density of a coloured dye image on the other hand will vary according to the colour of the light by which it is measured. To take a simple example, a yellow dye absorbs blue light but is almost completely transparent to light of other colours such as green and red. An image consisting of a yellow dyestuff thus has various densities to blue light but zero density all over to green and red light. In practice, even the best yellow dye will absorb a little green and red light but the absorption in these spectral regions is normally insignificant because it is so small.

Magenta dye has density to green light but it is fully transparent to blue and red light. Finally, cyan dye absorbs only red light and allows blue and green to pass freely. It is as well to point out that even the best magenta dyes absorb some of the blue light which they should transmit freely and that the best of cyan dyes have some density to green light and blue light. These shortcomings of the best available dyestuffs do not seriously affect the determination of exposures and filtering in colour printing and for purposes of explanations that follow it will be assumed that yellow dyes absorb only blue light, magenta only green and cyan only red light. (Figure 11.1).

A colour printing paper has three emulsion layers respectively sensitive to blue, green and red light. This means that the yellow image of the negative controls the exposure of the blue-sensitive paper layer and hence the density of the yellow image. In the same way the magenta image in the negative controls the density of the print magenta image and the cyan negative layer controls the density of the cyan image of the print.

If a colour negative is printed in the normal manner on to colour paper it is most unlikely that the densities of the three print images will be correct for neutral balance. Far more likely is a pronounced and objectionable colour cast. For neutral balance in a print the colour of the light source in the enlarger, the relative densities of the three images of the negative and the relative speeds of the paper layers must all be correctly related. If they are not, the result is a colour cast perhaps a very strong one.

Because of the variations in negatives, enlargers and printing papers a straightforward printing method is impracticable. Two methods are available for securing balanced colour prints, the additive and white-light methods. In the additive or tricolour system three separate exposures are given to the paper through tricolour blue, green and red filters respectively. The durations of the exposures govern the depth and colour balance of the print. By careful adjustment of the exposures a neutral print can be obtained from negatives having different blue, green and red light densities and on papers having layers of different speeds.

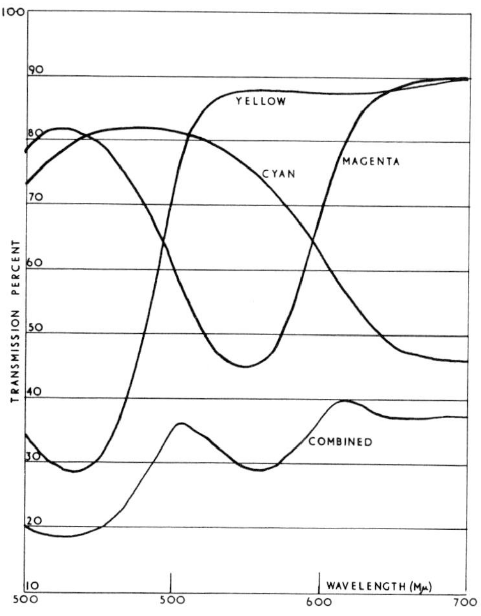

Fig. 11.1 Spectral transmittance curves of low densities of yellow, magenta and cyan dyes. The lower curve is that for the three layers superimposed. The visual colour was approximately neutral.

The white-light printing system is not well-named. It involves a single exposure but the colour of the exposing light is modified by placing a filter pack in the beam. The filters are chosen from a series of yellow, magenta and cyan filters of various densities. The filter pack adjusts the relative amounts of blue, green and red light in the exposing beam so that the three layers of the paper receive correct relative exposures.

CHAPTER TWELVE

COLOUR BALANCE IN PRINTS

To understand the principles of balancing colour prints it is necessary to look at the sensitometry of colour negative and print materials. In Figure 12.1 are shown the characteristic curves of a hypothetical colour negative film exposed to light for which it is balanced. The curves lie almost exactly one on top of the other which is indicative of perfect balance. Any subject recorded by the film under these conditions will show perfect balance in the negative. A scale of greys may not look neutral to the human eye but it will "look" neutral to a colour printing paper.

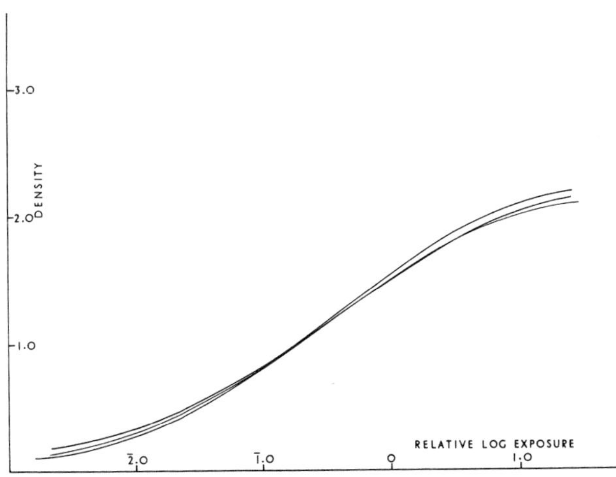

Fig. 12.1 Characteristic curves of a hypothetical colour negative film having no integral masks and exposed to light for which it is balanced.

Figure 12.2 shows the characteristic curves of a colour printing paper, again a hypothetical one. In this case the curves are not superimposed, indicating that the relative speeds of the three layers are not the same for the colour of light used for making the sensitometric exposure. This is not particularly important provided the speed differences are not extreme. They can be brought to equality by adjusting the relative amounts of blue, green and red light in the exposing illumination.

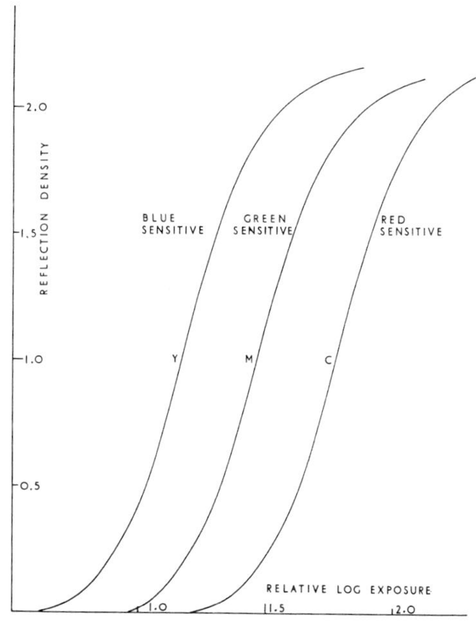

Fig. 12.2 Characteristic curves of a colour printing paper. The lateral displacement of the curves relative to each other indicate that the three layers have different speeds for the colour of the exposing illumination used.

In Figure 12.2 the curve for the blue-sensitive layer of the paper is displaced 0.6 log exposure units to the left of the red-sensitive layer and the curve for the green-sensitive layer is 0.3 log exposure units to the left of the red-sensitive curve. Thus, for the exposing source used, the blue-sensitive layer is 4 times faster than the red-sensitive layer and the green-sensitive emulsion is twice as fast as the red-sensitive layer.

These speed differences can be corrected only by slowing down the faster emulsions to match the slowest and to do this a yellow filter transmitting only 25 per cent of the blue light falling on it (density to blue light of 0.6) and a magenta filter absorbing 50 per cent of the green light (density to green light of 0.3) would have to be placed in the exposing beam.

Using the white-light method of exposing, a filter pack of a 60 yellow and a 30 magenta colour printing filters would be required for printing a perfectly balanced negative on the paper of which the curves are shown in Figure 12.1, using the same light source as that employed for plotting the characteristic curves of the paper.

Using the tricolour or additive method of exposing the print, the required adjustment of the relative speeds of the paper layers would be achieved by giving exposure times in the ratio of, Blue 1, Green, 2 and Red 4. This ratio would be upset by the fact that the tricolour filters do not transmit blue, green and red light completely. The blue filter in particular may transmit only 10 per cent of the blue light while the red filter is usually an efficient transmitter of red light. This does not however affect the principle that the three exposure times are adjusted in the manner described.

Assume that, using the appropriate tricolour printing filters and exposing source, a paper requires exposure times in the ratio of Blue 4, Green 3 and Red 2 to yield a set of characteristic curves like those in Figure 12.2. To correct the speed differences between the layers the exposure ratio would have to be altered to Blue 1, Green $1\frac{1}{2}$ and Red 2.

The characteristic curves of a colour negative film in Figure 12.1 represent the situation in which the material is perfectly balanced for the light source used eg. a film balanced for daylight exposed by a source operating at a colour temperature of 5,500 K. In practical photography this does not happen often. The balance of the film may not be perfect and the subject illumination may be of higher or lower colour temperature than that for which the film is designed. To take an extreme example, the film may be exposed to tungsten lighting with a colour temperature of say 3,000 K which is much lower than that of mixed sunlight and skylight at 5,500 K. The film curves will separate as shown in Figure 12.3 in which red-sensitive curve shows the highest speed and the blue-sensitive curve the lowest.

Colour negative films have large exposure ranges so that it is feasible to expose them to illumination for which they are not really balanced. A film that is balanced for daylight can be exposed by electronic flash having a colour temperature

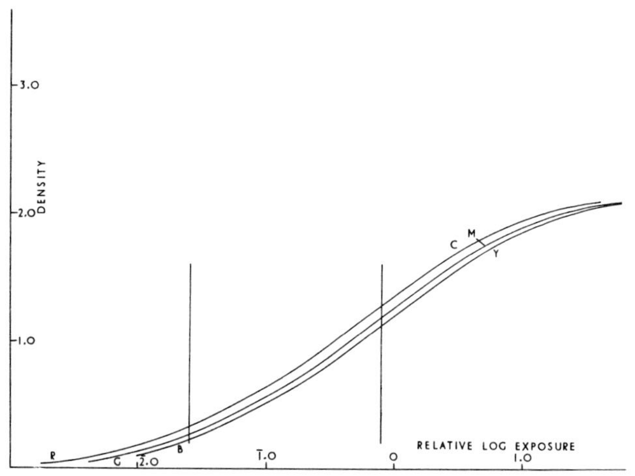

Fig. 12.3 Characteristic curves for an unmasked colour negative film balanced for daylight exposed to a tungsten source. The three emulsion layers can be seen to have different relative effective speeds.

of about 6,000 K and the lack of balance in the resulting negatives can be corrected perfectly at the printing stage. In Figure 12.3 the two vertical lines indicate the portions of the three characteristic curves likely to be utilized by a subject of average contrast when a daylight balanced film is exposed to tungsten illumination. In the resulting negative the yellow, magenta and cyan images will have different densities as can be seen, the cyan being the densest and the yellow the thinnest. If such a negative is printed using a filter pack calculated to bring just the paper into balance for the light source used for exposing it, the print will be seriously off-balance because of the different densities of the three images in the negative. The print image will be deficient in cyan and it will have a yellow image which is too dense. The colour cast will be orange-red.

The remedy here is to add further filters to the pack in the enlarger, yellow to increase the overall density of the yellow image in the negative and some magenta filtering to increase the density of the magenta image of the negative. As the camera exposure has avoided the toes and shoulders of all three curves of the film, such correction will be wholly effective. In tricolour printing the same correction would be achieved by reducing the blue filter exposure by a suitable amount and the green filter exposure by a smaller amount.

To revert to white-light exposures, the effect of additional filtering for the correction of an out-of-balance negative is to lift the two lower curves so that all three coincide. The filter pack in white-light colour printing may be regarded as having two components, one necessitated by the enlarger light source and the relative speeds of the three layers of the paper and the second component that may be required to correct the balance of the negative. The former remains constant until the enlarger light source or batch of paper is changed; the latter may alter from one negative to another but usually by small amounts. In tricolour printing the exposure ratios are affected partly by the light source and paper batch and partly by the balance of the negative.

Correction of faulty negative balance is completely effective only if the toes and shoulders of the film curves are avoided as shown in Figure 12.3. Had the camera exposure been inadequate as shown in Figure 12.4 an insoluble problem would have arisen. Filtering added to the pack to correct the negative balance fails to make the portions of the curves utilized to coincide throughout their lengths. We have the phenomenon of what is called, "the filter printing through the shadows". The shadows in the print take on a cast complementary in hue to that of the added filters. In the case quoted the cast would be bluish.

Exactly the same thing happens in tricolour printing although here the balance correction is effected by increasing the red and green filter exposures or decreasing the blue and green filter exposures.

To avoid problems like this which admit of no solution when once the negative has been exposed, it is essential to use suitable filters on the camera lens when exposing a negative film by subject illumination for which it is not balanced. This moves the curves of the faster film layers to the right by the correct amount to bring them all to the same effective speed. These matters are however beyond the scope of this book but film makers' literature gives filter recommendations for various exposing conditions.

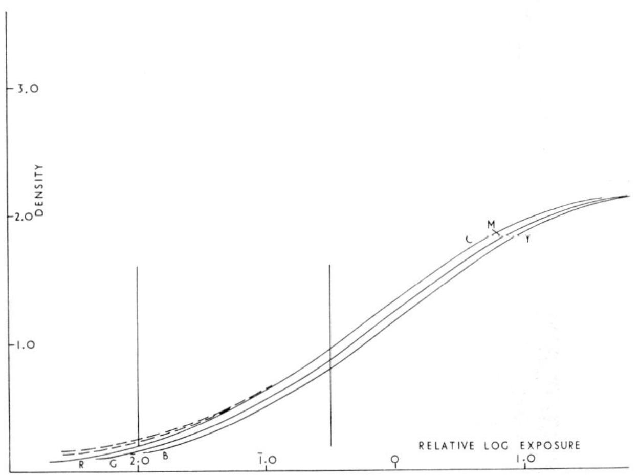

Fig. 12.4 An under-exposed colour negative that is out of balance cannot be corrected fully by modifying the printing filter pack. The curves are no longer superimposed throughout their lengths.

The characteristic curves of colour negative film reproduced to aid explanations all relate to unmasked film. Most negative films today contain integral coloured masks designed to minimise the imperfections of the best available magenta and cyan dyes. The characteristic curves of such films are separated in a vertical direction, that for the blue-sensitive layer being at the top and the curve of the red-sensitive layer at the bottom as shown in Figure 12.5. The three curves should be parallel throughout their lengths and for perfect balance they

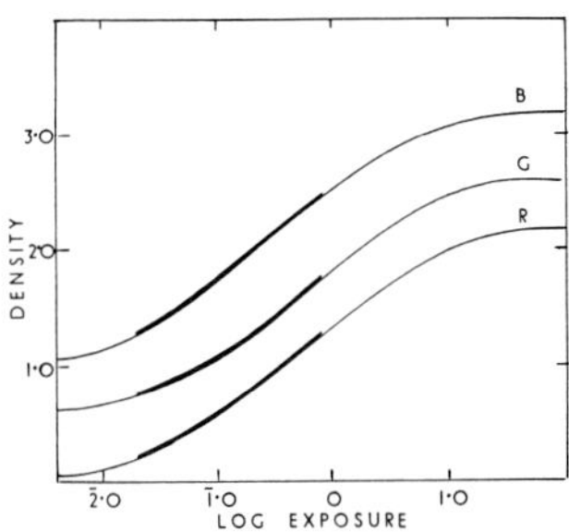

Fig. 12.5 Characteristic curves of a colour negative film having integral coloured masks. These have the effect of separating the curves vertically but this has no important sensitometric significance.

should not be displaced laterally with respect to each other. The presence of masking in no way invalidates the sensitometric principles already discussed.

CHAPTER THIRTEEN

PRINCIPLES OF COLOUR DENSITOMETRY

We can measure the densities of yellow, magenta and cyan dye layers simply by using light of a colour which the dye absorbs. This is blue for the yellow dye, green for the magenta dye and red for cyan dye. The required colour of light is obtained by placing filters in the light beam of the densitometer. Most commercial densitometers are fitted with filters in a slide or a turret so that any one of the filters can be moved into the light beam at will.

Some of the more advanced densitometers are arranged so that the photocell and filter unit can be placed on the enlarger easel for on-easel evaluation of colour negatives.

In the same way that the total density of a black and white negative can be measured as explained in an earlier chapter, so can the colour total densities of colour negatives be measured by placing filters in the light beam. We have the same choice in colour printing between spot and integrating photometry. The former is the more precise but it calls for more sensitive and expensive equipment.

If the density of a small area or the whole of a colour negative is measured to blue light, the value obtained is essentially the blue light density of the yellow image as both magenta and cyan dyes are perfectly transparent to blue light, at least theoretically. Because practice in this case does not meet the theoretical requirements completely, the blue light density includes the unwanted blue light densities of the magenta and cyan images as well. Such colour densities are known as "integral" densities. It is, of course, such integral densities that are the effective values in colour printing.

The green light densities are those of the magenta image and densities measured by red light are the red light densities of the cyan layer. Here again the unwanted absorptions of the magenta and cyan dyes are being disregarded although they will not be disregarded by the densitometer.

It is desirable to have a suitable reference surface included in every colour negative. The professional photographer is better able to arrange this than the amateur when he is using a 4 x 5 in. technical camera or larger. An 18 percent reflectance neutral grey card is available from Messrs. Kodak Ltd. and it is usually feasible to include this somewhere in the subject just inside the field of view. Its image in the negative must be large enough to be measureable with the densitometer available but $\frac{1}{8}$ in. square is generally big enough. The reference surface must also be lit to the same level and by the same colour of light as the rest of the subject and it must be positioned so that it does not have light reflected on it from nearby brightly-coloured surfaces.

An alternative reference surface for subjects containing human models is a flesh tone but the use of such a tone means that flesh will be rendered as the same hue in all prints whether the model is a glamorous blonde or a sun-tanned seaman. Flesh cannot therefore be regarded as being a satisfactory reference surface as a grey card but it is useful if a grey is not available.

If an integrating method of colour negative evaluation is used there is no need for a reference surface but it is still worth having one for assessing the colour print and in case a change is made later to small area negative evaluation. The integrating method of negative evaluation is based on the assumption that all scenes integrate to neutral grey. Quite surprisingly the majority of scenes do but there are exceptions such as the close-up of the girl in a scarlet sweater the latter taking up a substantial proportion of the negative area. This gives rise to what is called "subject failure" and a print balanced on the basis of its integrated blue, green and red light transmissions will show a cyan cast, the colour of the cast being complementary to that of the predominant subject colour.

There are many sets of tricolour filters available. These are dense blue, green and red filters such as are required for colour densitometry but the choice of the most appropriate set is a matter of some importance and no little difficulty. Ideally, their peak transmissions should coincide with the peak absorptions of the negative dyes and these absorptions should, in turn, agree with the sensitivity regions of the three paper layers.

The photographer should follow the recommendations of the makers of the negative and paper materials he uses. If he prints negatives of one maker on paper by another he may be in difficulties that can be solved only by trial and error. For Kodak materials such as Kodacolor-X and Ekta-color films type S and type L printed on Ektacolor paper the Wratten filters Nos. 92, 93 and 94 are recommended and many commercial densitometers are fitted with these. Agfa-Gevaert Ltd. do not seem to favour colour negative evaluation

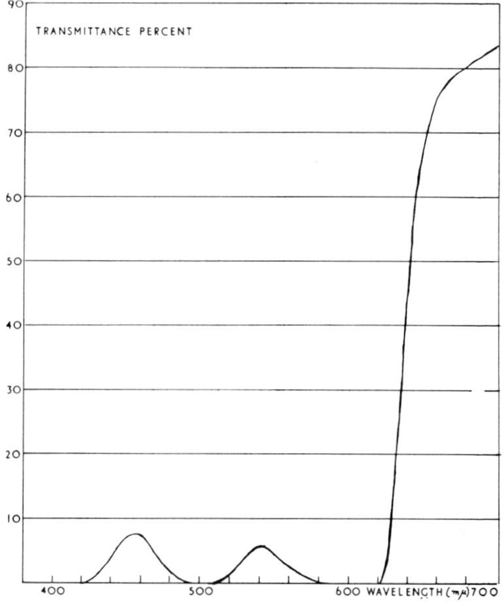

Fig. 13.1 Spectral transmittance curves for Wratten filters nos. 92, 93 & 94.

by measurement and make no specific filter recommendations for colour densitometry. Many workers find that the Wratten set gives good results with Agfacolor materials.

As tricolour filters transmit freely in the infra-red, an infra-red rejection filter should be used in the densitometer when measuring Kodak colour negatives. A colourless heat-absorbing glass filter has been found effective. An ultra-violet absorbing filter such as the Wratten No. 2B should also be present in the light beam although this is merely a precaution that is probably unnecessary as tricolour filters all absorb U.V. effectively.

There is a wide range of densitometers which can be used for the measurement of integral colour densities. Some are primarily black and white instruments that can be adapted to colour work while others have been developed expressly for colour negative evaluation and the designers have set out to obtain the high sensitivity required when using narrow-cut tricolour filters in the light beam.

Possibly the least expensive of all instruments is the Kodak colour densitometer. Its low price — about fifty pounds — is explained by the fact that it is a visual comparator with which the unknown density is compared with the continuously variable densities of a calibrated annular wedge. It is a suitable densitometer for those who lack the capital to invest in a complex electronic densitometer costing several hundreds of pounds. It can be used for the measurement of reflection colour densities as well as transmission densities.

The Kodak instrument is supplied with a metal slide carrying a set of glass tricolour filters any one of which can be introduced into the light beam as required. Any visual comparator is tiring to use for long series of measurements and with increasing fatigue comes decreasing matching accuracy. When measuring through the blue filter which is visually denser than the other two, the field illumination drops to a low level and matching accuracy at high densities is decreased. In spite of this it is a useful device for the colour photographer who prefers measurement to guesswork.

The Baldwin transmission densitometer is well-known in Britain and it is used in conjunction with the Baldwin photometer Mk 34 which comprises an emissive photocell and a stable D.C. amplifier. The high sensitivity of the photometer enables the densest of the tricolour filter sets to be used but the density range covered is restricted if the smallest sample aperture supplied is used.

Direct current amplifiers are notoriously unstable but the Baldwin photometer is satisfactory in this respect provided it is switched on about half an hour before it is used. It should be left switched on throughout the day unless it is to be out of use for considerable periods.

The Baldwin densitometer is fitted with a filter slide with four circular apertures taking glass or gelatine filters 1 in. in diameter. These can be equipped with a set of tricolour filters such as the Wratten Nos. 92, 93 and 94. If desired, the fourth aperture in the filter slide can be provided with a photopic filter for measuring visual black and white densities. This filter adjusts the effective spectral sensitivity of the photocell to match that of the average human eye.

A Baldwin reflection densitometer is available which is also used in conjunction with the Baldwin photometer Mk 34. It has a turret for the accommodation of tricolour filters and with it, the reflection colour densities of prints can be measured.

The Macbeth series of "Quantalog" densitometers are designed with colour work very much in mind. They make use of a photomultiplier in conjunction with an A.C. amplifier

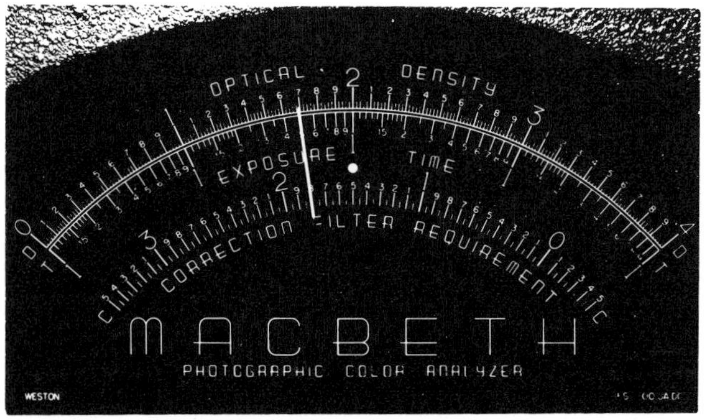

Fig. 13.2 Scale of Macbeth "Quantalog" EP–1000 showing the density scale, scale for filter pack estimation, and exposure time scales.

and they are extremely sensitive instruments capable of measuring small areas of high density even when using narrow-cut tricolour filters. The "Quantalog" densitometers are provided with additional scales designed to facilitate the calculation of filter packs in colour printing and the Model EP—1000 is equipped with "memory" circuits in which can be stored the balance data for one or more standard negatives. Such refinements do not add to the accuracy of measurements but they make for rapid working.

Macbeth densitometers are manufactured in USA and are costly in Britain. They are marketed by Messrs. Johnsons of Hendon Ltd. The "Photolog" densitometer is similar in appearance to the "Quantalog" is manufactured in Britain

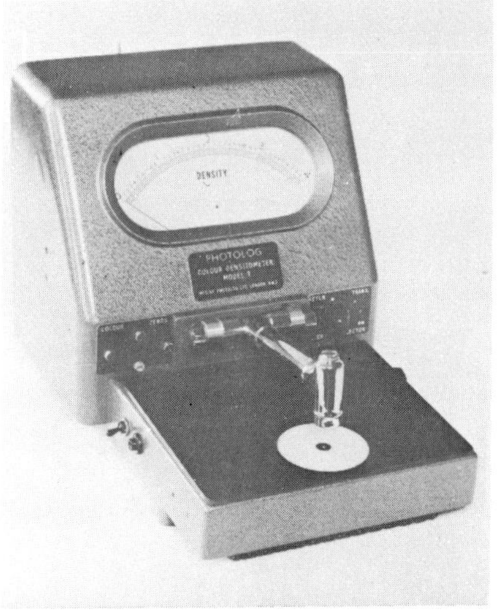

Fig. 13.3 Photolog colour densitometer Model T. This is a British made instrument very suitable for off-easel evaluation of colour negatives.

and is relatively inexpensive. It incorporates fibre optics and a reflection head is available as an accessory. The light-sensitive element is a photomultiplier and A.C. amplification is used.

The EEL colour densitometer Model 103 is different from most of the other instruments on the market. The photo-sensitor is a selenium photocell and its output, without amplification, is measured by a highly sensitive galvanometer giving full-scale deflection at only 0.75 microamperes. The absence of amplification restricts the overall sensitivity to the extent that the Ilford standard tricolour filters are fitted. These are not ideal because of their wide transmissions but it has been found that in the evaluation of colour negatives and similar work, the use of non-ideal filter sets may introduce only trivial errors.

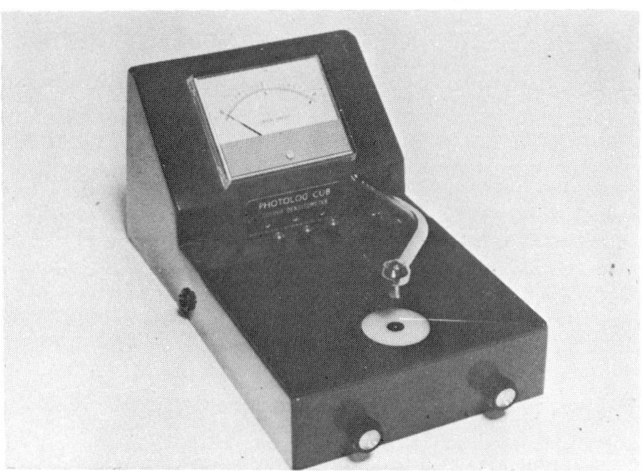

Fig. 13.4 Photolog digital densitometer.

There is a wide range of colour densitometers on the American market. They differ in detail with regard to methods of use in colour printing and many of them offer facilities for on-easel measurement of the image. This enables filter packs to be calculated and also printing exposure times. If the exposure time is known for a particular negative, filter pack and degree of enlargement and the light intensity in the exposing plane has been measured and recorded, measurement of the light intensity on the easel from an unknown negative with its filter pack enables the new exposure time to be calculated. The colour densitometer may have an additional scale of relative exposure times to facilitate such calculations.

Such exposure estimations can be made either on the basis of spot evaluation of the image of a grey card or by integration of the whole image. The latter method is less reliable but it is the only one available if the negative being printed has no suitable reference tone.

Table of commercial colour densitometers and colour analysers for on-easel evaluation. The list is not exhaustive but it includes most of the best-known instruments.

Name	Types	Manufacturer
Quantalog	Transmission and reflection densitometers and also on-easel analysers	Macbeth Instrument Corporation, Newburgh, New York, U.S.A.
Gretag	Transmission and reflection densitometers	Gretag Ltd., Zurich, Switzerland.
Baldwin	Transmission and reflection densitometers	Baldwin Instrument Co., Dartford, England.
Densichron	Transmission and reflection densitometers	Welch Scientific Co., Shokie, Illinois, U.S.A.
Colour Densitometer Model 133	Transmission densitometer. Reflection attachment available as an accessory	Evans Electroselenium Ltd., Halstead, Essex, England.
Photolog	Transmission and reflection densitometers and also on-easel colour analysers	Photolog Ltd., 32–34 Gordon House Road, London N.W.5.

Many of the above manufacturers make also densitometers for black and white measurements only.

CHAPTER FOURTEEN

EVALUATION OF COLOUR NEGATIVES

In discussions of negative evaluation it is necessary to consider separately the two methods available for exposing the colour printing paper. There is the tricolour or additive method calling for three separate exposures through blue, green and red filters. This means that a suitable set of filters has to be fitted in front of the enlarger lens in such a way that they can be changed between exposures without risk of moving the enlarger and causing lack of registration of the three print images.

Makers of colour printing paper specify sets of filters suitable for the tricolour exposure of their material. Kodak Ltd. supply the Wratten Nos. 99, 98 and 70 for their Ektacolor paper (Figure 14.1). Agfa-Gevaert Ltd. recommend their filters Nos. B478A, G527A, and R678 (Figure 14.2). The Paterson colour print kit includes a set of filters the transmissions of which are shown in Figure 14.3.

The balance and depth of a colour print is controlled by the relative and absolute values of the three exposure times. If the exposures required to produce a good print from a standard negative are known, the exposures needed for a print from an unknown negative can be worked out from the colour densities of the two negatives. It is assumed that both the standard and the unknown negative include a reference grey area. If this is not so then a flesh tone or other reference area will have to be used.

Suppose that the standard negative calls for tricolour filter exposures as follows —

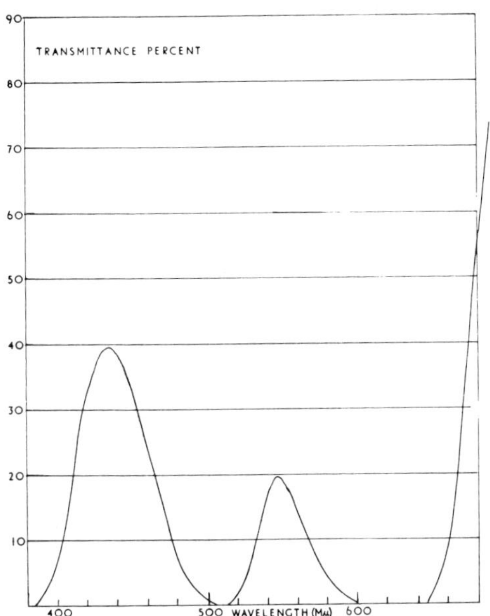

Fig. 14.1 Spectral transmittance curves for the Wratten tricolour printing filters Nos. 99, 98 and 70.

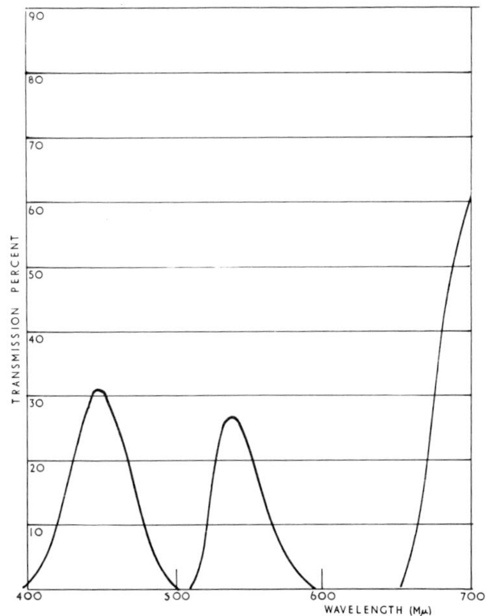

Fig. 14.2 Spectral transmittance curves for the Agfa-Gevaert tricolour filters B478A, G527A and R678.

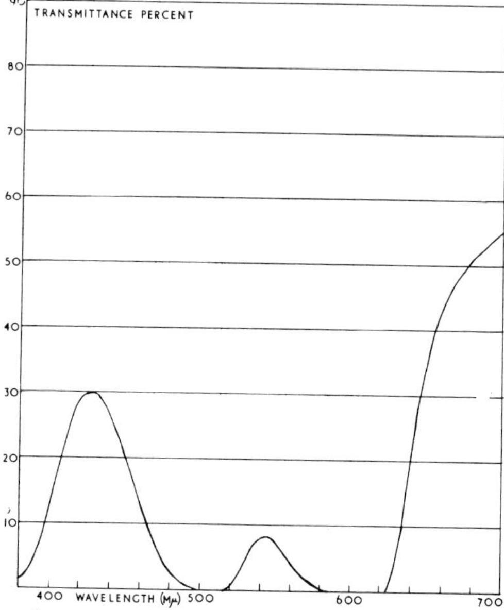

Fig. 14.3 Spectral transmittance curves for the Paterson tricolour printing filters.

B	G	R
20 sec	18 sec	12 sec

Suppose also that colour density measurements of the image of the reference area yield the following values —

B	G	R
1.4	1.15	0.97

In printing a new negative the tricolour densities are measured and their values might be —

B	G	R
1.25	1.25	0.80

To find the new exposure times it is necessary to work out the three density differences, giving them positive or negative values depending on whether the new density is higher or lower than that of the standard negative, thus —

B	G	R
−0.15	+0.10	−0.17

By finding the antilogarithms of these density differences we arrive at factors by which the exposure times required by the standard negative have to be multiplied or divided to give the exposure times for the new negative. A positive density difference becomes a multiplying factor and a negative difference a dividing factor. In the present example the factors are as follows —

B	G	R
÷1.4	x 1.26	÷1.5

Making use of these factors the exposure times for the new negative become —

B	G	R
20 ÷ 1.4 = 14 sec	18 x 1.26 = 23 sec	12 ÷ 1.5 = 8 sec

These calculations may look a little forbidding but they are worked quite quickly in practice.

It is worth noting that in the tricolour system the working out of the exposure times for an unknown negative automatically ensures a print of suitable depth unless the subject is one that demands a darker or lighter print than usual. With the white-light system the calculation of filter pack changes does not give the new exposure time. This has to be worked out as a separate operation.

In white-light printing a single exposure is given to the paper and the colour of the enlarger illumination is modified by means of a filter pack made up from a set of yellow, magenta and cyan filters of various densities. At no time is it necessary to use filters of all three colours in a pack as such a pack contains unnecessary and undesirable neutral grey which has the effect of increasing the duration of the printing exposure but with no effect on colour balance.

Several makers offer sets of colour printing filters in gelatine film or acetate foil and the Kodak colour printing (CP for short) filters are the best known and the most useful as their numbers are related to their densities. Each of the three colour series is numbered thus, 025, 05, 10, 20, 30, 40 and 50. A decimal point placed in front of these numbers gives the density of the filter concerned to light of the colour it absorbs. A 20Y filter thus has a density of 0.20 to blue light.

Kodak Ltd. measure these filters with a spectrophotometer and it does not follow that measurements with a transmission densitometer fitted with the tricolour filters used for evaluating colour negatives will give exactly the same values. This is of little consequence and the user can calibrate his own set of filters using the same densitometer and filters as used for measuring his colour negatives. The higher values of the Kodak CP filters are numbered according to their actual densities as well as carrying their nominal numbers. Thus a 40 filter may carry the number $37\frac{1}{2}$ or $42\frac{1}{2}$ indicating that its actual density is closer to 0.375 or 0.425 than to 0.40.

The equivalent Agfa-Gevaert colour printing filters are numbered 05, 10, 20, 30, 40, 50 and 99 and there are two 99 filters of each colour in a set. Appearances suggest that the numbering of these filters follows the Kodak system but the numbers are purely arbitrary and do not relate to density except that the higher the number the darker the filter. It is up to the individual to calibrate his own set of filters and to assign them new numbers accordingly.

In the table below are measurements for typical sets of Kodak CP and Agfacolor printing filters measured with a transmission densitometer fitted with the Wratten filters Nos. 92, 93, and 94. An infra-red rejection filter was fitted to the densitometer when measuring the Kodak filters but it was discarded for the Agfacolor set. Agfacolor paper sensitivities extend into the near U.V. and I.R.

Effective Densities of Colour printing Filters

Agfa-Gevaert Printing Foils

Measured with Baldwin transmission densitometer with Wratten filters Nos. 92, 93 and 94. No ultra-violet or infra-red absorbing filters.

Filter Number	Density		
	Yellow	Magenta	Cyan
05	.05	.06	.07
10	.09	.08	.11
20	.14	.14	.19
30	.18	.20	.24
40	.22	.24	.35
50	.24	:31	.40
99	.46	.58	.76

Kodak Colour Printing Filters (CP)

Measured with Baldwin transmission densitometer with Wratten filters Nos. 92, 93 and 94. Wratten 2B filter and Ilford 803 (infra-red absorbing) filter in light beam.

Filter Number	Density		
	Yellow	Magenta	Cyan
025	.06	.08	.025
05	.09	.10	.07
10	.12	.12	.10
20	.21	.21	.18
30	.30	.26	.26
40(37½)	.375	.34	.32
50	.42	.40	.38

The lack of close agreement between the nominal values of the CP filters and the density values obtained is no reflection on the filters. The discrepancies result from the inevitable differences between various methods of measurement. Nevertheless, such measured values obtained by the individual with his own densitometer are the ones to use.

As in tricolour printing, a balanced print has to be made from a standard negative finding the filter pack and exposure required by trial and error. This operation provides the data required for working out the filter pack and exposure for a print from an unknown negative. If the standard negative is measured using the included grey patch as a reference surface the densitometer readings might be as follows —

B	G	R
1.52	1.31	1.11

For the purpose of discussion it will be assumed that the standard negative required a filter pack of 60Y + 35M. For the moment the exposure time required by the print from the standard negative can be ignored as it is irrelevant as far as filter pack calculations are concerned.

Measuring the colour densities of an unknown negative let it be assumed that the following values are obtained —

B	G	R
1.41	1.46	1.01

The two sets of density readings reveal that the yellow image of the new negative is less dense than that of the standard negative. The magenta image is denser and the cyan image is thinner. These differences can be stated in the following form —

B	G	R
+0.11	−0.15	+0.10

In this case the densities of the new negative are subtracted from those of the standard and if the difference is a positive one it means that filtering has to be added to the pack, if it is negative, filters must be subtracted from the pack. The change in filter pack therefore resolves itself to —

+10Y	−15M	+10C

The changes must be added to the existing filter pack of 60Y + 35M, —

Y	M	C
60	35	
+10	−15	+10
70	20	10

The new pack contains filters of all three colours and the unwanted neutral can be eliminated by subtracting a value of 10 from all three colours leaving a final pack of 60Y + 10M.

Change of filter pack means a change in exposure as a rule and the table below gives the factors for the Kodak CP filters. These are applied by dividing the exposure time for the standard negative by the appropriate factor for every filter removed from the pack and multiplying the result by the factors for every new filter added to the pack. These factors take into account not only the absorptions of the filters but also the loss of light by reflection from the surfaces.

An alternative method is to work in filter densities which can be added and subtracted instead of having to be multiplied or divided. The table below gives the effective densities of the Wratten CP filters. The densities of the filters in an existing pack are added together and so are the densities of all the filters in a new pack. The two totals are subtracted from each other and the antilogarithm found of the answer. This is the factor by which the exposure has to be changed and if the new pack has a higher total density than the existing one the factor is used as a multiplier. If, on the other hand, the new pack has a lower density than the original one then the old exposure is divided by the factor to find the new time.

Factors and Densities of Kodak Colour Printing Filters

Filter	D	F	Filter	D	F	Filter	D	F
CP 025Y	0.07	1.2	CP 025M	0.08	1.2	CP 025C—2	0.08	1.2
CP 05Y	0.07	1.2	CP 05M	0.09	1.2	CP 05C—2	0.08	1.2
CP 10Y	0.07	1.2	CP 10M	0.11	1.3	CP 10C—2	0.08	1.2
CP 20Y	0.07	1.2	CP 20M	0.16	1.4	CP 20C—2	0.08	1.2
CP 30Y	0.08	1.2	CP 30M	0.21	1.6	CP 30C—2	0.11	1.3
CP 37½ Y			CP 37½ M			CP 37½ C—2		
CP 40Y	0.08	1.2	CP 40M	0.26	1.8	CP 40C—2	0.15	1.4
CP 42½ Y			CP 42½ M			CP 42½ C—2		
CP 47½ Y			CP 47½ M			CP 47½ C—2		
CP 50Y	0.08	1.2	CP 50M	0.30	2.0	CP 50C—2	0.17	1.5
CP 52½ Y			CP 52½ M			CP 52½ C—2		

Kodak Ltd. added a red series (now discontinued) to their CP filters having the same numbers as the other colours. The factors and densities of the red filters can be taken as being the same as those for the magenta filters. The cyan filters listed in the above table are the series 2 which is an improvement on the original CP cyan filters which they replace and which had slightly higher densities.

In working out exposures it is essential to consider the number of filters in a pack as well as their values. Filtering of say, 70Y could be made up in a variety of ways such as 50Y + 20Y, 40Y + 20Y + 10Y, or 42½ Y + 20Y + 05Y + 025Y. The values all total 70Y but the increase in exposure required by the last combination would be greater than that for the first simply because of the number of actual filters involved.

Kodak Ltd. publish a data sheet, CL–13 covering the estimation of printing exposures when changing filter packs and this includes a useful nomogram for use with CP and CC filters. The latter, colour compensating filters, are very similar to CP filters but they are of high enough optical quality to be used in an image-forming light beam. The CP filters are designed for use only between the light source and the negative in an enlarger and not between the negative and the printing paper.

An additional correction has to be made to a printing exposure time, if, in working out a new filter pack, a neutral component is eliminated. This was the case with the example given on the previous page. The overall density of the new filter pack and negative is 0.10 less than the standard negative and its filter pack. The newly calculated exposure time should therefore be divided by the anti-logarithm of 0.10 i.e. 1.26. This is seen to be necessary if the tricolour densities of the two negatives and their packs are added together thus —

	B	G	R
Standard negative	1.52	1.31	1.11
Filter pack	0.60	0.35	0
	2.12	1.66	1.11
New negative	1.41	1.46	1.01
Filter pack	0.60	0.10	0
	2.01	1.56	1.01

It would be quite possible to have two negatives of identical balance but of different densities. These would require the same filter pack but different exposure times for the same magnification and lens aperture. In working out the change in filter pack required in substituting one of these negatives for the other in the enlarger the calculation would involve removal of unwanted neutral from the new filter pack in the case where the new negative is less dense than the one already printed. We should arrive back at the same filter pack and hence there would appear to be no need to change the exposure time. There would be however because of the lower overall density of the new negative.

In arriving at a filter pack, density differences have to be rounded off to suit available filters. A density difference of 0.06 has to be corrected by an 05 filter and so forth. Any error arising will be too small to be seen in the resulting print.

If in working out changes in filtering on the basis of negative evaluation it is found that a certain value of one of the filters should be removed from the existing pack and there is none to remove, the difficulty is overcome by adding the same value of filters to the other two colours. Thus, if it is necessary to remove 20C from a pack consisting of 60Y + 35M we add 20Y and 20M to make the final pack 80Y + 55M.

At this stage it may be advisable to re-state the principles of colour cast correction of prints made from colour negatives. To remove a cast, filters of the same colour as the cast must be added to the filter pack, or filters complementary to the cast must be removed. The stronger the cast the deeper the filters needed to eliminate it. In tricolour printing the principles are similar but the rule is that to reduce or eliminate a cast of a particular hue, the exposure must be reduced to light of colour complementary to the cast. Thus a yellow cast calls for a reduction in the blue filter exposure and a red cast necessitates giving less exposure through both the blue and green filters. If a print has say a yellow cast but is not dark enough it would be foolish to reduce the exposure through the blue filter. It would be better to increase the green and red exposures to produce more magenta and cyan to remove the yellow cast and to darken the whole print at the same time.

Although measurement is of inestimable help in arriving at a neutral colour balance in prints it should be supplemented by visual assessment of test exposures as well. If calculation indicates that an increase in yellow filtering is required or a reduction of the blue light exposure and a trial exposure shows a noticeable bluish cast, then there is something wrong with the measurements or arithmetic somewhere and the error must be found and corrected.

Positive-positive colour processes are becoming increasingly popular. Reversal duplicating film is available for making copy transparencies from original transparencies and reversal colour paper for making prints direct from colour transparencies. The principles of colour negative evaluation apply equally to the evaluation of colour transparencies for making copies or direct prints. In making visual assessments of trial exposures on duplicating film or reversal paper however, it is essential to remember that the correction of colour casts is the reverse of that in negative-positive printing. A yellow cast, for example, calls for an *increase* in the blue-filter exposure in tricolour printing or the *removal* of yellow filters from the filter pack in white-light printing. This can be confusing especially if negative-positive and positive-positive processes are operated concurrently.

The calculations required for working out filter packs are the same in positive/positive working as in negative/positive and exposure calculations are the same also. It has to be borne in mind always that, in exposing a reversal material, a final image that is too light indicates over-exposure and one that is too dark results from under-exposure.

It is likely that the use of duplicating film and reversal paper will increase in the future. At the present time, the colour quality obtainable with them is not of the highest. Reversal colour prints and duplicate transparencies are second-generation colour photographs and tend to suffer from loss of colour saturation.

CHAPTER FIFTEEN

INTEGRATED COLOUR NEGATIVE EVALUATION

The alternative to spot densitometry for the evaluation of colour negatives is the overall or integrated measurement of the blue, green and red light transmissions of a negative. This system can be used where there is no suitable reference patch in the negative. As stated previously, the method is based on the assumption that all subjects integrate to neutral grey and this is true enough for integrating densitometry to work. That it does work is demonstrated by the fact that it is used on rollhead colour printers in colour photofinishing and the colour balance obtained from correctly exposed negatives can be very good indeed.

Subject failure was mentioned briefly in an earlier chapter and it arises where a subject has a predominantly large area of saturated colour. The author saw recently a professionally made print of a retriever dog against a background of deep blue sky. The poor dog was quite yellow because of subject failure which produces a cast complementary in hue to the predominant subject colour.

Consider a scene in which a large area of brilliant blue appears. This area will be reproduced as yellow in the negative and the integrated green and red light densities of the negative will be unduly low as a result. Measurement will indicate the need for putting magenta and cyan filters into the pack or reducing the green and red light exposures for the tricolour system. In both cases there will be a deficiency of magenta and cyan in the print which means a yellow cast.

Subject failure to any serious extent is encountered more

rarely than might be thought. One reason for this is that few of the colours in nature are highly saturated. A large expanse of green grass might be thought to introduce subject failure but the greens of grass and foliage are very desaturated and are unlikely to give rise to a magenta cast unless they occupy a very large area of a negative indeed.

One advantage of total density measurement of colour negatives is that it can be done with relatively simple and inexpensive equipment. The densitometer embodying a Weston Master exposure meter described in Chapter 8 and illustrated on page 82, can be used for evaluating colour negatives as well as for the estimation of exposure times in black and white enlarging. This necessitates making provision for locating tricolour filters in the light beam and in the photograph of the densitometer the accommodation for these is indicated. The filters themselves, of gelatine film, are carried in a cardboard mount as shown in Figure 15.1. The notches in the edge of the mount are for the purpose of locating each of the three filters accurately in front of the photocell window of the meter. A lightly spring-loaded plunger made of three-ply and let into the side of the meter housing of the optical bench engages with the notches in the filter mount.

A more powerful light source is required for colour negative evaluation than for black and white negative measurements and a No. 1 photoflood lamp of the colour temperature controlled variety gives adequate light. The colour temperature controlled photoflood is preferable to the ordinary type as it is a little less overrun and has slightly longer and more consistent light output. It operates at a colour temperature of 3,200 K. instead of the usual 3,400 K.

If Kodak colour negative materials are being measured, an infra-red absorbing filter should be placed just below the meter window. Colourless or pale blue heat-absorbing glass appears to be adequate for this purpose and the author has used the Ilford filter No. 802 or 803 successfully. This absorbs infra-red and some of the deep red. An ultra-violet absorbing filter such as the Wratten No. 2B can also be included. Such a filter has to be used in the enlarger when printing on Ektacolor paper by the white-light method and while tricolour filters absorb U.V. there are some tricolour blue filters that transmit down to 360 millimicrons. For Agfacolor negative both the infra-red and U.V. absorbing filters should be discarded.

Any on-easel evaluation equipment can be used by the integrating method even if it is designed for the measurement of small areas in the image. All that is required is a diffusing screen of matt plastic sheet or ground glass to place

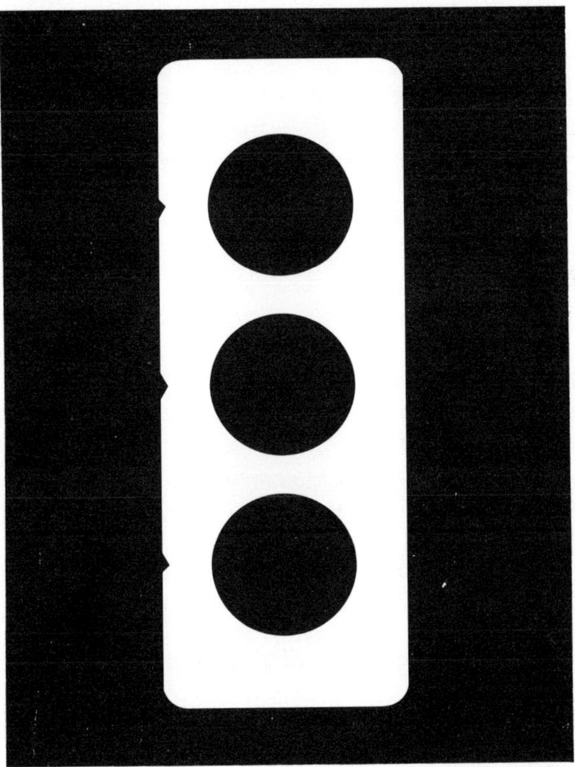

Fig. 15.1 Tricolour filters mounted for use in home-made densitometer embodying a Weston Master exposure meter. The notches at the edge ensure accurate location of each filter in the light beam.

in front of the enlarger lens while measuring to scramble the light. The diffusing material used must be an efficient scatterer of light so that no hint of subject detail or colour can be seen in the light falling on the easel. The material should also be colourless and as few materials are perfectly so it is as well to use one particular diffuser always and not to change from plastic to ground glass and back again. Ground glass is usually slightly greenish and matt plastic may be yellowish and the change in colour, small as it is, can give rise to errors.

The same general procedure is used for calculating tri-colour exposure times and filter packs when employing integrating evaluation as when measuring the small area of a grey card image or other reference surface. A standard negative is required from which a good print has been produced as the result of trial exposures. The standard negative is then measured, either on or off the easel, and the data obtained are used along with similar data for an unknown negative. The calculations involved are just the same as those described in Chapter 14.

When evaluating a negative as a whole it is essential that none of the rebates is included in the measurements. These have no bearing on colour balance but they will affect the readings obtained. In the case of negatives with integral coloured masks, inclusion of the orange-coloured rebates will tend to produce results based on a neutral balance for the film base rather than for the image. An absolutely opaque mask around the negative image will exclude the rebates and the mask aperture can be made a little smaller than the image for the sake of safety.

An interesting approximate method of evaluating the image of a colour negative on the enlarger baseboard is provided by the Theilgaard calculator supplied with the Paterson colour print kit. It consists of a trio of identical small step-wedges each overlaid with one of the tricolour filters, blue, green and red. The wedges are mounted in a card-board paper holder taking a piece of colour paper about 2 x 3 in. The wedge steps are numbered from 1 to 48 and the numbers represent exposure times in seconds. The times are based on a trial exposure time of 30 seconds.

In use, a small piece of printing paper is placed in the holder and an exposure of 30 seconds given with a matt plastic scrambler over the enlarger lens. The negative has, of course, been focussed in the usual manner. On processing the paper, images of the wedges in yellow, magenta and cyan are revealed. The number visible in the faintest discernible step in each case is the exposure time required for the print through the corresponding filters. The yellow wedge indicates the blue filter exposure, the magenta wedge the green exposure and the cyan wedge the red filter exposure.

This is a simple but very ingenious device that is ideal for preliminary. tests under unknown printing conditions. It brings one within easy striking distance of a balanced print and, quite often, a first-off print is completely satisfactory.

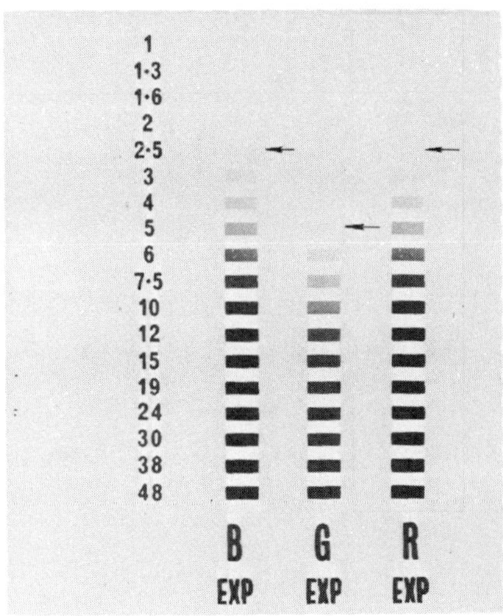

Fig. 15.2 The result of exposing a sample of paper behind the Paterson Theilgaard tricolour exposure estimator. In this example the exposure times indicated by the test are B 2½ sec, G 5 sec and R 2½ sec.

Subject failure affects results just as it does any integrating method of evaluation.

Although this calculator is designed for use with the tricolour exposure method it can be adapted to the white-light method. This calls for some simple preliminary calculations but these are worth doing especially when embarking on white-light printing for the first time when one may have no idea at all of the filter pack that may be required.

The colour model of the "Melico" enlarging exposure meter/timer can be used for on-easel evaluation of colour negatives and the instruction manual accompanying the instrument gives detailed directions for doing this. It is used by the integrating method or for spot measurement as may be appropriate.

CHAPTER SIXTEEN

USING A COLOUR INTEGRATING DENSITOMETER

A colour densitometer based on a Weston exposure meter is easy to use. It is set up with its light source and set of tricolour filters and a mask of suitable size for the negatives being measured located on the stage. At no time must the lamp be switched on without one of the tricolour filters in place in front of the cell window of the meter. The light from a photoflood so close to the meter can wreck the delicate moving coil movement because of the sudden violent swing of the needle. It would not be difficult to fit a micro-switch in the lamp circuit which is closed only when the tricolour filter mount is in position in its slide.

The lamp-to-meter distance should be adjusted so that, with the blue filter in the beam, full-scale needle deflection is obtained. This is easily achieved with most tricolour filter sets but it may prove difficult with the blue filter Wratten No. 94 because it is very dense. It may be necessary to be content with a maximum deflection less than full-scale but this is unimportant, and a deflection of exactly 8 on the low light scale of the Weston Master V will be found adequate. It is desirable to keep the photoflood lamp as far as possible from the glass negative stage in order to avoid thermal fracture or excessive heating of colour negatives.

With the blue filter giving full-scale deflection or nearly so, the green and red filters will give more than full-scale deflection with no negative on the stage. There is no danger of damage to the movement of the meter under these circumstances as it is designed to withstand the excessive needle deflection that must result if the baffle is inadvertently opened in bright sunlight. In use, excessive needle deflection is unlikely to occur often as there will normally be a negative on the stage.

If 35 mm negatives are being evaluated the smaller area of the mask aperture used will mean that the biggest deflection obtainable with the blue filter in the beam may be rather restricted. This cannot be helped but if blue readings are found difficult to determine accurately because they fall low on the scale, it may be worth using a non-ideal filter set. This may give better results because of the improved reading accuracy obtained with it.

Whenever the densitometer is used it is desirable to bring the needle deflection with the blue filter in the beam always to the same mark on the scale. This gives a constant reference point with which all readings can be kept relatively correct.

If a colour negative is now placed on the stage and the three filters brought in turn in front of the meter window, three different needle deflections will be obtained. These are a measure of the relative blue, green and red light transmissions and densities of the negative. For tricolour printing it is the relative transmissions that are more meaningful but for white-light printing relative densities are easier to calculate with.

An immediate problem arises in that the scale of a Weston meter is not designed for this present purpose and a scale chart is required for converting needle deflections into numbers relating to negative transmissions or densities. The low light scale of the Weston has undergone changes from model I to model V. All models prior to the V were scaled in actual units of brightness — candles per square foot — models I to III inclusive were scaled 0 to 50 candles per square foot and model IV, 0 to 25 candles per square foot on the low light ranges. With model V, actual units were abandoned in favour of arbitrary numbers 0 to 10. Fortunately, the scale itself has changed only from white on black to black on white — negative to positive!

A scale chart for tricolour printing has to be calibrated in relative light values and a suitable chart is shown in Figure 16.1. This particular chart is applicable to the

Weston Master IV and V and the original arbitrary numbers are shown on the chart. For white-light printing it is more useful to have a scale chart calibrated in logarithmic numbers like the negative indices proposed in Chapter 8 and such a chart, again for the Weston IV and V, is reproduced in Figure 16.2. A difference of one number on the scale is equivalent to a 10 CP filter and it is possible to read the meter scale to within an 025 filter. A practical suggestion is to use a watchmakers' magnifier for reading the meter scale itself, especially down towards the lower light values where the divisions become somewhat crowded. Tricolour and white light scale charts for Weston meters I, II and III are shown in Figures 16.3 and 16.4.

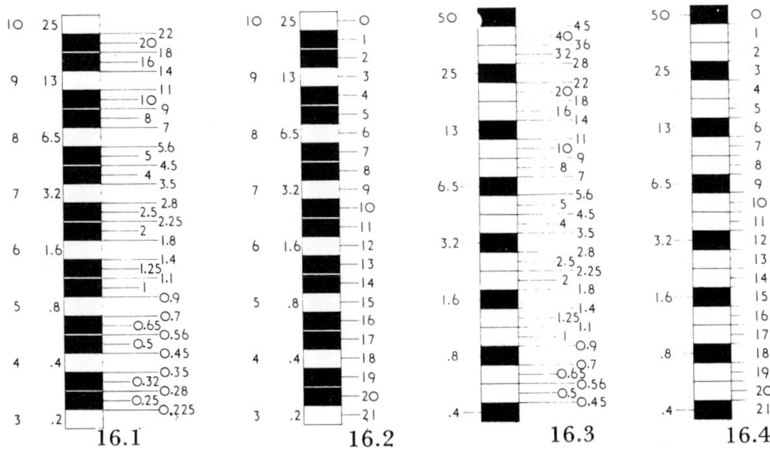

Fig. 16.1 Scale chart for Weston Master meters IV and V for use in tri-colour printing.

Fig. 16.2 Scale chart for Weston meters IV and V for use in white light printing.

Fig. 16.3 Scale chart for tricolour printing for use with Weston Master meters I, II, and III.

Fig. 16.4 Scale chart for white light printing with Weston meters I, II and III.

In colour printing all density readings relating to negative evaluation should be recorded, either in a notebook reserved for the purpose, or on dockets that can be filed with negatives for future reference. Calculations on odd scraps of paper can become mislaid and this makes it impossible to check them in the event of a suspected error. The author went to some trouble to design dockets suitable for both tricolour and white-light printing. These were drawn on white paper with indian ink, lettering being done with "Uno" stencils. Reflex document copy negatives were made from the originals and transmission contact prints on document paper were made from the negatives. Although this was a more elaborate system than was strictly necessary it was conducive to orderly working which is one of the secrets of successful colour printing.

If prints are being made by the tricolour method the first print from a standard negative provides a set of light value readings from the negative and a set of exposure times. The following figures will serve as a working example —

	B	G	R
Light values for standard negative	0.8	14	25
Exposure times for standard negative	20 sec	32 sec	25 sec

If it is now wished to print an unknown negative, its relative light transmissions are measured and recorded, thus —

	B	G	R
Light values for unknown negative	1.1	9	22

The exposure times required by the unknown negative are found by simple proportion —

$$\text{Blue exposure} = 20 \times \frac{0.8}{1.1} = 14 \text{ seconds}$$

$$\text{Green exposure} = 32 \times \frac{14}{9} = 51 \text{ seconds}$$

$$\text{Red exposure} = 25 \times \frac{25}{22} = 28 \text{ seconds}$$

In deciding whether a particular exposure should be increased or decreased it should be remembered that an increase in light value calls for a decrease in exposure time and vice versa.

Like black and white paper, colour paper suffers from low-intensity reciprocity failure and big changes in the lengths of exposure times from one print to another should be avoided if possible. Also, if the exposure time through a particular filter has to be increased or decreased by a factor of 2 or more, the calculated exposure times may not be quite correct.

In white-light printing the same setting-up procedure is used starting with the best possible print from a standard negative, finding the filter pack by means of test strips. For this let a filter pack of 55M + 15C be assumed and densitometer readings of —

B	G	R
17	15	9

The unknown negative is measured and let the readings for it be —

B	G	R
$18\frac{1}{2}$	13	$9\frac{1}{2}$

The differences required in the filter pack are found by subtracting the readings of the unknown negative from those of the standard negative —

B	G	R
17	15	9
$18\frac{1}{2}$	13	$9\frac{1}{2}$
$- 1\frac{1}{2}$	$+ 2$	$- \frac{1}{2}$

The plus and minus signs indicate addition or removal of filters and the above differences can now be converted into CP filter numbers —

$-15Y$	$+20M$	$-05C$

Combining the filter pack with the above differences —

	55M	15C
$-15Y$	$+20M$	$-05C$
$-15Y$	75M	10C

As there are no yellow filters in the pack for the standard negative the $-15Y$ can be dealt with only by adding 15 filtering to the magenta and cyan filters which gives a final pack of 90M + 25C.

It must be emphasised that all the numerical examples given may bear little relationship to actual values obtained in practice. The figures have been chosen to show as clearly as possible the principles involved in the simple calculations. Another point worth making is that the scale chart for white-light printing can be numbered in many different ways. Here it has been suggested that a series of numbers starting at zero be used, the higher the number the higher the density and a difference of 1 in. reading to be equivalent to a number 10 CP filter. It may be preferred to use a series of numbers in which an interval of 1 is equivalent to an 05 filter. If tricolour and white-light printing methods are both in use, it may seem more logical to reverse the series of numbers so that a high number means a **high** light transmission and low density instead of the other way round. Any of these variations, and others, are permissible and provided the methods of calculation are geared to the scaling of the meter chart, the correct answers will emerge.

Although it is possible to calculate the new exposure time required in white-light printing by taking into account changes in the filter pack and the density of the new negative, there is a rather quicker and more reliable method that can be employed with the integrating densitometer. It involves measuring the light transmission or density of the standard negative and its filter pack and carrying out the same measurement with an unknown negative and its pack. Increased needle deflection for the unknown negative indicates the need for reducing the exposure time and if the deflection is less, the exposure has to be increased. The amount of the exposure decrease or increase can be determined by the change in needle deflection. A change corresponding to one number — a 10 CP filter — means an exposure factor of $\sqrt[3]{2}$ (1.26). A two-number change is equivalent to a factor of 1.6 and a change of three numbers indicates a factor of 2. For a negative denser than the standard the factor is applied by multiplication and for a thinner negative the exposure time is divided by the factor.

APPENDIX 1
LOW INTENSITY RECIPROCITY FAILURE OF PRINTING PAPERS

Recent investigations into low intensity reciprocity failure of present-day printing papers have revealed that the magnitude of failure is often much greater than might be suspected. Furthermore, it varies considerably from one paper to another and even between samples of the same paper of different batches. An example of such variation is shown in Figure Ap. 1.1. The two curves are for two different batches of the same grade and make of glossy bromide papers and the curves show the exposure time required to produce a mid-tone density plotted against the exposure time calculated on the basis of the illumination on the paper.

These are probably extreme examples but they are actual examples and the data for the two curves were obtained by the most rigorous experimental methods. Generally speaking, enlarging exposure times lie in the region of 1 to 30 seconds and for most papers the effect of low-intensity reciprocity failure is small within this range. There are however the exceptional cases in which exposure times of several minutes may be required and reciprocity failure cannot be ignored. Any compensation built-in to an enlarging photometer will be for average reciprocity failure and cannot therefore be relied on implicitly.

It is worth pointing out that it is often possible to keep enlarging exposure times fairly constant by making full use of lens apertures. For example, suppose that a negative has been enlarged with the lens stopped down to f/8 and that a photometer has indicated an exposure time of 10 seconds for the grade of paper being used. For subsequent negatives it may be feasible to leave the photometer set for the previous negative and to manipulate the lens apertures to adjust the light on the photocell to produce a balance as shown by the neon or meter. This is, in fact, a null-reading method which always has much to commend it. It eliminates errors due to non-linearity of the instrument as the latter

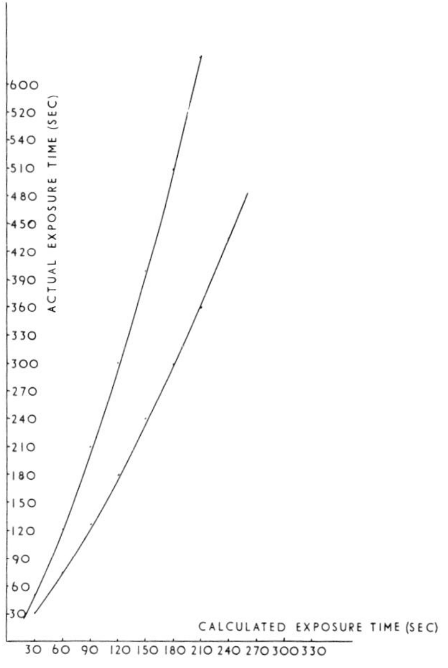

Fig. Ap. 1.1 Showing the low-intensity reciprocity failure character-istics of two different batches of the same normal grade of bromide paper.

is being used only for indicating identity of two light intensities.

When enlarging a mixed lot of negatives to various magnifications, it is impossible to maintain the same exposure time throughout but if the principle is observed, it is feasible to avoid unduly large variations and so to avoid serious exposure errors arising simply because of low-intensity reciprocity failure.

Low-intensity reciprocity failure in colour printing papers is made complicated by the fact that there are three emulsions instead of one. All three suffer from reciprocity failure but the magnitude of the failure varies from one layer to another. This means that if a balanced print is produced at an exposure of say 10 seconds, and another print is made from the same negative and with the same filter pack but at a greater magnification so that a much longer exposure time has to be given, it is unlikely that the second print will be in balance.

It is important therefore to determine filter packs with this fact in mind. If a big change in exposure time has to be made, a trial exposure is desirable. From the trial, small adjustments can be made to the pack to correct any colour cast that has resulted from differential reciprocity failure.

A manufacturer of a colour printing paper is able to offer recommendations with regard to any exposure increase required when the calculated exposure time is unduly long but any change in balance can be discovered only by making a test exposure. As far as possible, exposure times should be kept as constant as possible by making use of the apertures on the enlarging lens. There is a limit to this, of course, but it may be possible to divide the negatives to be printed into groups on the basis of their densities and the degree of enlargement they are to receive.

The table below is suitable for use with Ektacolor Commercial paper but it should be used only as a guide.

EKTACOLOR PAPER

Exposure time corrections for low intensity reciprocity failure

Ratio of new to old Exposure time	Factor	Ratio of new to old Exposure time	Factor
1.1	1.02	3.1	1.25
1.2	1.04	3.2	1.26
1.3	1.05	3.3	1.27
1.4	1.07	3.4	1.28
1.5	1.08	3.5	1.29
1.6	1.10	3.6	1.29
1.7	1.11	3.7	1.30
1.8	1.13	3.8	1.31

Table (*cont.*)

Ratio of new to old Exposure time	Factor	Ratio of new to old Exposure time	Factor
1.9	1.14	3.9	1.31
2.0	1.15	4.0	1.32
2.1	1.16	4.1	1.33
2.2	1.17	4.2	1.33
2.3	1.18	4.3	1.34
2.4	1.19	4.4	1.35
2.5	1.20	4.5	1.35
2.6	1.21	4.6	1.36
2.7	1.22	4.7	1.36
2.8	1.23	4.8	1.37
2.9	1.24	4.9	1.37
3.0	1.25	5.0	1.38

The figures in the above table should be regarded only as a guide. To use them, divide the shorter of the two exposures into the longer to find the exposure ratio. If the new exposure is longer than the old use the factor as a multiplier; if it is shorter the factor should be divided into the new exposure time.

Example A colour print is made that requires an exposure time of 20 seconds. Another negative is printed and the calculated exposure is 60 seconds. Dividing the smaller into the larger gives 3 as a result. In the table the exposure factor for a ratio of 3 is 1.25 so the calculated 60 seconds must be multiplied by 1.25 which gives an answer of 75 seconds.

FILTERS FOR COLOUR DENSITOMETRY

Because there are several sets of different tricolour filters that may be used in a densitometer for the evaluation of colour negatives, five different sets were tested in the author's optical bench fitted with a Weston Master exposure meter. These included the standard tricolour set with over-lapping transmissions, the set recommended for use in tri-colour printing on Ektacolor paper, the filters from the Paterson Colour Print kit, Wratten filters Nos. 92, 93 and 94, and a set of old Pakolor filters. The last were included because they were the original filters used in the testing of the evaluation method based on total density. A standard and an unknown negative were measured with each filter set and the change in filter pack indicated was worked out. The results are set out in the table below. Although the filter pack changes vary they are all in the same direction. A filter pack change of +15M +20C proved to be satisfactory.

When the tricolour method of printing is employed it is reasonable to conclude that the actual printing filters should be used for negative evaluation. No matter what the spectral absorption characteristics of the negative dyes, it is only the light transmitted by the printing filters that is effective.

Filters		Blue	Green	Red
Wratten 25, 58 & 47B	Standard neg.	$11\frac{1}{2}$	5	$2\frac{1}{2}$
	New neg.	$11\frac{1}{2}$	$3\frac{1}{2}$	0
			+15M	+25C
			15M plus	25C
Wratten 98, 99 & 70	Standard neg.	12	$7\frac{1}{2}$	9
	New neg.	$12\frac{1}{2}$	6	7
		−05Y	+15M	+20C
			20M plus	25C
Paterson Printing filters	Standard neg.	10	6	4
	New neg.	$10\frac{1}{2}$	$4\frac{1}{2}$	$1\frac{1}{2}$
		−05Y	+15M	+25C
			20M plus	30C
Wratten 92, 93 & 94	Standard neg.	17	12	5
	New neg.	17	$10\frac{1}{2}$	3
			+15M	+20C
			15M plus	20C
Pakolor Printing filters	Standard neg.	11	$6\frac{1}{2}$	$2\frac{1}{2}$
	New neg.	$11\frac{1}{2}$	$4\frac{1}{2}$	$\frac{1}{2}$
		−05Y	+20M	+20C
			25M plus	25C

All readings taken with No. 1 photoflood with colourless heat-absorbing glass and no U.V. absorber.

INDEX